Manifest

Your Desires

Other Hay House Titles by Esther and Jerry Hicks
The Teachings of Abraham®

Books, Calendar, and Card Decks

The Law of Attraction (available in Spanish)
The Amazing Power of Deliberate Intent (also available in Spanish)
Ask and It Is Given (also available in Spanish)
Ask and It Is Given Cards
Ask and It Is Given Perpetual Flip Calendar
The Astonishing Power of Emotions (available in Spanish in 2009)
The Law of Attraction Cards
Money, and the Law of Attraction
(book; 5-CD set—both available August 2008)
Relationships, and the Law of Attraction
(book; 5-CD set—both available April 2009)
Sara, Book 1: Sara Learns the Secret about the Law of Attraction
Sara, Book 2: Solomon's Fine Featherless Friends
Sara, Book 3: A Talking Owl Is Worth a Thousand Words!
(available April 2008)
Spirituality, and the Law of Attraction
(book; 5-CD set—both available October 2009)
The Teachings of Abraham Well-Being Cards

Additional CD Programs

The Teachings of Abraham Master Course Audio (11-CD set)
The Law of Attraction (4-CD set)
The Law of Attraction in Action (2-DVD set)
The Amazing Power of Deliberate Intent (Parts I and II: two 4-CD sets)
Ask and It Is Given (Parts I and II: two 4-CD sets)
The Astonishing Power of Emotions (8-CD set)
Sara, Book 1 (unabridged audio book; 3-CD set)

DVD Programs

The Law of Attraction in Action, Episodes I, II, III, IV, V (2-DVD set)
The Teachings of Abraham Master Course Video (5-DVD set)
The Secret Behind "The Secret"? (Abraham) (2-DVD set)

crosses

Please visit Hay House USA: **www.hayhouse.com**®
Hay House Australia: **www.hayhouse.com.au**
Hay House UK: **www.hayhouse.co.uk**
Hay House South Africa: **www.hayhouse.co.za**
Hay House India: **www.hayhouse.co.in**

Manifest Your Desires

365 Ways to Make Your Dreams a Reality

HAY HOUSE, INC.
Carlsbad, California • New York City
London • Sydney • Johannesburg
Vancouver • Hong Kong • New Delhi

ESTHER AND JERRY HICKS

THE TEACHINGS OF ABRAHAM®

Published and distributed in the United States by: Hay House, Inc.: www.hayhouse.com • *Published and distributed in Australia by:* Hay House Australia Pty. Ltd.: www.hayhouse.com.au • *Published and distributed in the United Kingdom by:* Hay House UK, Ltd.: www.hayhouse.co.uk • *Published and distributed in the Republic of South Africa by:* Hay House SA (Pty), Ltd.: www.hayhouse.co.za • *Distributed in Canada by:* Raincoast: www.raincoast.com • *Published in India by:* Hay House Publishers India: www.hayhouse.co.in

Editorial supervision: Jill Kramer • *Design:* Amy Gingery
Illustrations: Kristina Swarner

The material in this book was adapted from the *Ask and It Is Given Perpetual Flip Calendar* © 2007 by Esther and Jerry Hicks • Published by Hay House, Inc.

Library of Congress Control Number: 2006937215

ISBN: 978-1-4019-1694-7

11 10 09 08   4 3 2 1
1st edition, June 2008

Printed in China

Introduction

We've put together this information-packed little book, which presents the teachings of the Non-Physical entity **Abraham,** to help you learn how to manifest your desires so that you're living the joyous and fulfilling life you deserve.

Each day you'll come to understand how your relationships, health issues, finances, career concerns, and more are influenced by the Universal laws that govern your time-space reality—and you'll discover powerful processes that will help you go with the positive flow of life.

So start making your dreams a reality . . . right now!

— Esther and Jerry Hicks

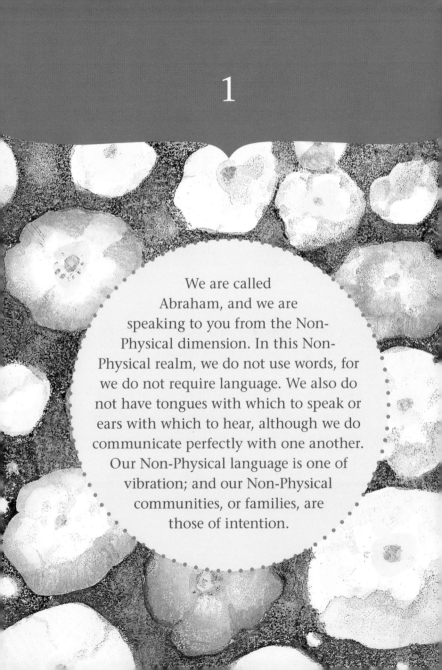

1

We are called
Abraham, and we are
speaking to you from the Non-
Physical dimension. In this Non-
Physical realm, we do not use words, for
we do not require language. We also do
not have tongues with which to speak or
ears with which to hear, although we do
communicate perfectly with one another.
Our Non-Physical language is one of
vibration; and our Non-Physical
communities, or families, are
those of intention.

2

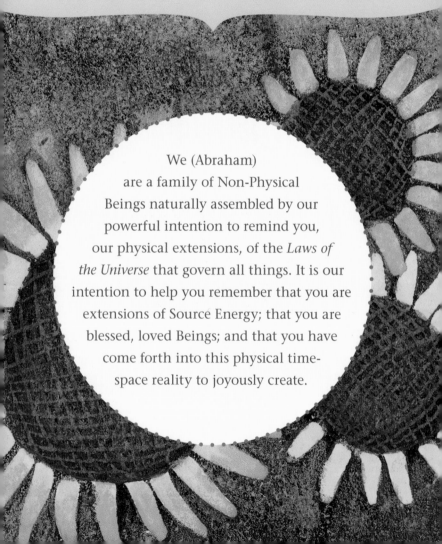

We (Abraham)
are a family of Non-Physical
Beings naturally assembled by our
powerful intention to remind you,
our physical extensions, of the *Laws of
the Universe* that govern all things. It is our
intention to help you remember that you are
extensions of Source Energy; that you are
blessed, loved Beings; and that you have
come forth into this physical time-
space reality to joyously create.

3

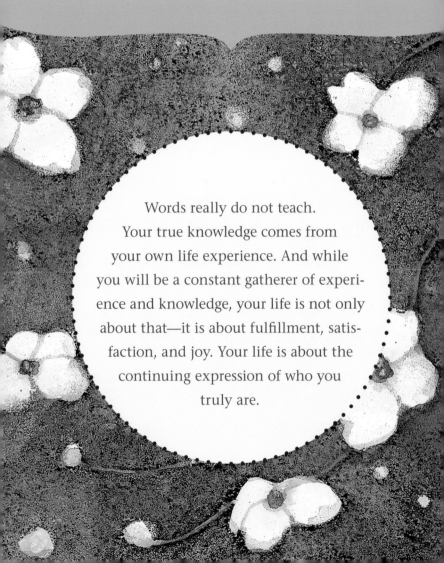

Words really do not teach.
Your true knowledge comes from
your own life experience. And while
you will be a constant gatherer of experience and knowledge, your life is not only
about that—it is about fulfillment, satisfaction, and joy. Your life is about the
continuing expression of who you
truly are.

4

We are communicating
with you at many levels of your
awareness, all at the same time, but
you will only receive whatever you are
now ready to receive. Everyone will not
get the same thing from this material, but every reading will net you
something more.

5

Do you know what you want?
Are you enjoying the evolution of
your desire? If you are among the
rare humans who answered, "Yes, I'm
enjoying the evolution of my desire,"
then you understand who you are and
what this physical life experience is
really all about.

6

You said, "I will
go forth into the physical
time-space reality among other
Beings, and I will assume an identity
with a clear and specific perspective."
You said, "I will love pouring myself into
this physical body, into physical time-
space reality, for that environment will
cause me to focus the powerful Energy
that is me into something more specific. And in the specifics of that
focus, there will be powerful
motion forward—
and joy."

There is nothing that you cannot be, do, or have; and we want to assist you in achieving that. But we love where you are right now, even if you do not, because we understand how joyful the journey to where you want to go will be.

8

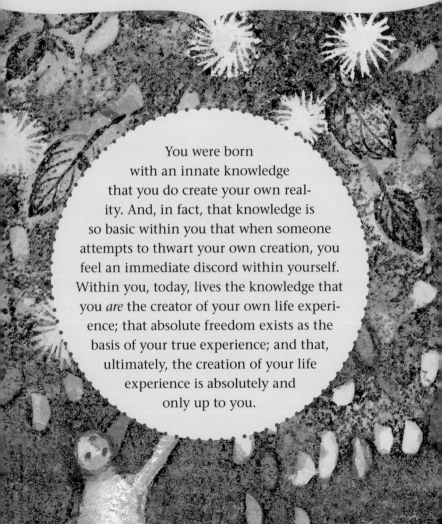

You were born
with an innate knowledge
that you do create your own reality. And, in fact, that knowledge is
so basic within you that when someone
attempts to thwart your own creation, you
feel an immediate discord within yourself.
Within you, today, lives the knowledge that
you *are* the creator of your own life experience; that absolute freedom exists as the
basis of your true experience; and that,
ultimately, the creation of your life
experience is absolutely and
only up to you.

These Teachings
of Abraham are written to
assist you in consciously returning
to the knowledge that you are free and
that you always *have been* free—and that
you always *will be* free to make your
own choices. There is no satisfaction in
allowing someone else to attempt to
create your reality. In fact, it is not
possible for anyone else to
create your reality.

You are an
Eternal Being who has
chosen to participate in this specific physical life experience for many
wonderful reasons. And this time-space
reality on planet Earth serves as a plat-
form in which you are able to focus your
perspective for the purpose of specific
creation. You are Eternal Consciousness,
currently in this wonderful physical
body for the thrill and exhilara-
tion of specific focus and
creation.

11

These Teachings
of Abraham are written
to help you understand that you
have the ability to always allow your
true nature to pour through you, and that
as you learn to *consciously* allow your full
connection with the You that is your Source,
your experience will be one of absolute joy.
By consciously choosing the direction of
your thoughts, you can be in constant
connection with Source Energy, with
God, with joy, and with all that
you consider to be good.

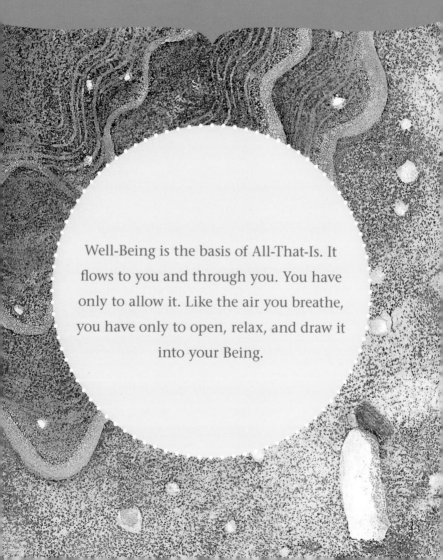

Well-Being is the basis of All-That-Is. It flows to you and through you. You have only to allow it. Like the air you breathe, you have only to open, relax, and draw it into your Being.

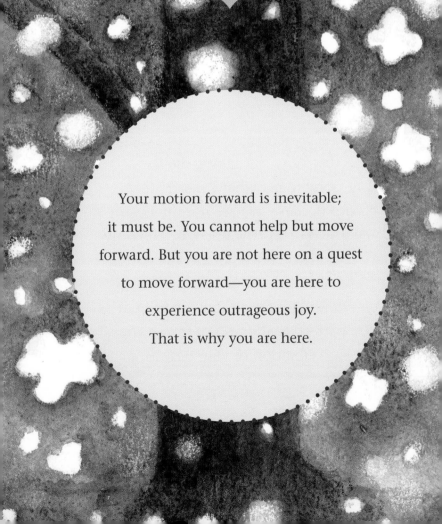

13

Your motion forward is inevitable;
it must be. You cannot help but move
forward. But you are not here on a quest
to move forward—you are here to
experience outrageous joy.
That is why you are here.

"Why is it taking me so long to get what I want?" It is not because you are not intelligent enough or worthy enough. The only reason you have not already gotten what you desire is because you are holding yourself in a vibrational pattern that does not match the vibration of your desire.

15

Gently and
gradually, piece by piece,
release your resistant thoughts,
which are the only disallowing fac-
tors involved. Your increasing relief
will be the indicator that you are
releasing resistance, just as your feelings of increased tension, anger, frustration, and so on have been your
indicators that you have been
adding to your resistance.

Well-Being is lined up outside your door. Everything you have ever desired, whether spoken or unspoken, has been transmitted by you vibrationally. It has been heard and understood by Source and has been answered, and now you are going to *feel* your way into allowing yourself to receive it, one feeling at a time.

17

Everything in your
physical environment was
created from a Non-Physical
perspective by that which you call
Source. And just as Source created you
and your world—through the power of
focused thought—you are continuing to create your world from your
Leading Edge place in this
time-space reality.

You and that which you call
Source are the same. You cannot
be separated from Source. When
we think of you, we think of Source.
When we think of Source, we think
of you. Source never offers a thought
that causes separation from you.

Source is always fully available to you, and Well-Being is constantly extended to you; and often you are in the state of *allowing* this Well-Being, but sometimes you are not. *We want to assist you in <u>consciously</u> allowing your connection, more of the time, to Source.*

As extensions
of Non-Physical Energy,
you are taking thought beyond
that which it has been before—and,
through contrast, you will come to
conclusions or decisions. And once you
align with your desire, the Non-Physical
Energy that creates worlds will flow
through you . . . which means
enthusiasm, passion, and
triumph. That is your
destiny.

From the Non-Physical,
you created you; and now from
the physical, you continue to create.
We all must have objects of attention
and desires that are ringing our bells in
order to feel the fullness of who we are
flowing through us for the continu-
ation of All-That-Is. That desire is
what puts the eternalness in
eternity.

Do not
underestimate the value of
your preferences, for the evolution
of your planet depends upon those
of you on the Leading Edge of thought
continuing to fine-tune your desires.
And the contrast, or variety, provides
the perfect environment for the
formation of your personal
preferences.

As you are standing in the midst of contrast, new desires are radiating constantly from you in the form of vibrational signals that are received and answered by Source—and, in that moment, the Universe is expanding. . . . These teachings are not about the expanding Universe, or about Source answering your every request, or about your worthiness—for all of that is a given. They are about you putting yourself in a vibrational place of receiving all that you are asking for.

You *do* create your own
reality. No one else does. And you
create your own reality even if you do
not understand that you do so. For that
reason, you often create by default. *When
you are consciously aware of your own thoughts
and are deliberately offering them, then you are
the <u>deliberate</u> creator of your own reality—*
and that is what you intended when
you made the decision to come forth
into this body.

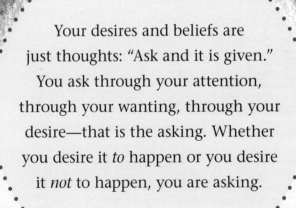

Your desires and beliefs are just thoughts: "Ask and it is given." You ask through your attention, through your wanting, through your desire—that is the asking. Whether you desire it *to* happen or you desire it *not* to happen, you are asking.

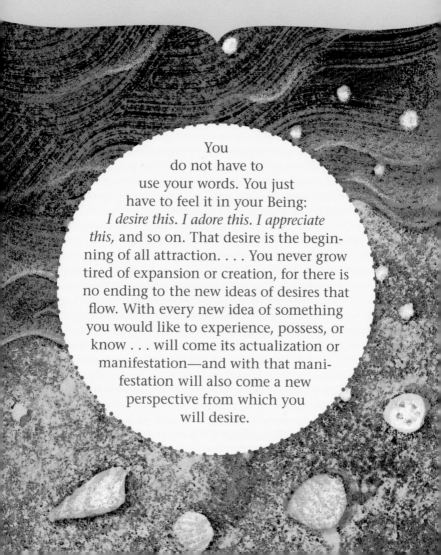

You
do not have to
use your words. You just
have to feel it in your Being:
*I desire this. I adore this. I appreciate
this,* and so on. That desire is the beginning of all attraction. . . . You never grow
tired of expansion or creation, for there is
no ending to the new ideas of desires that
flow. With every new idea of something
you would like to experience, possess, or
know . . . will come its actualization or
manifestation—and with that manifestation will also come a new
perspective from which you
will desire.

The contrast, or variety,
never ends, so the sprouting
forth of new desires will never end;
and as that "asking" never ends, the
"answering" never ceases to flow. And
so, new contrasts, and new inspiring
desires and perspectives, will be
laid out eternally before you.

You will never cease to be;
new desires will be constantly
born within you; Source will never
stop answering your desires; and your
expansion is, therefore, eternal. And
so, you may begin to relax if, in this
moment, there is something that
you desire that has not yet come
to fruition.

It is our desire
that you become one who
is happy with that which you
are and with that which you have—
while at the same time being eager
for more. That is the optimal creative
vantage point: To stand on the brink of
what is coming, feeling eager, optimistic
anticipation—with no feeling of impa-
tience, doubt, or unworthiness hindering the receiving of it—that is
the *Science of Deliberate
Creation* at its best.

30

There is a current that runs through everything. It exists throughout the Universe, and it exists throughout All-That-Is. It is the basis of the Universe, and as you begin to understand this basis of your world and begin to *feel for* your awareness of this Source Energy that is the basis of all things, you will then more clearly understand everything about your own experience and the experiences of those around you.

Like learning to understand the basics of mathematics and then having the successful experience of understanding the results of their applications, once you have a formula for understanding your world that is always consistent, it will yield consistent results to you.

32

You are, even
in your physical expres-
sion of flesh, blood, and bone,
a "Vibrational Being"; and everything you experience in your physical
environment is vibrational. And, it is
only through your ability to translate vibration that you are able to
understand your physical
world at all.

Your eyes, your
ears—even your nose,
tongue, and fingertips—are
translating vibrations . . . but your
most sophisticated of vibrational interpreters by far are your emotions. By
paying attention to the signals of your
emotions, you can understand, with
absolute precision, everything
you are now living or have
ever lived.

By paying atten-
tion to the way you feel,
you can fulfill your reason for
being here, and you can continue
your intended expansion in the joyful
way that you intended. By understanding your emotional connection to who-
you-really-are, you will come to understand not only what is happening in
your own world and why, but you
will also understand every other
living Being with whom
you interact.

35

Every thought vibrates, every thought radiates a signal, and every thought attracts a matching signal back. We call that process the *Law of Attraction*. The *Law of Attraction* says: *That which is like unto itself, is drawn.*

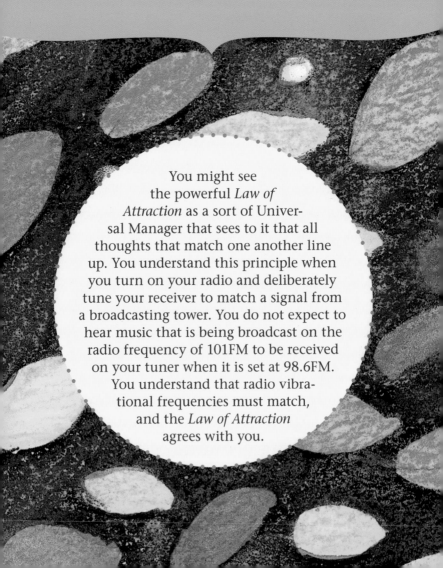

You might see
the powerful *Law of
Attraction* as a sort of Universal Manager that sees to it that all
thoughts that match one another line
up. You understand this principle when
you turn on your radio and deliberately
tune your receiver to match a signal from
a broadcasting tower. You do not expect to
hear music that is being broadcast on the
radio frequency of 101FM to be received
on your tuner when it is set at 98.6FM.
You understand that radio vibrational frequencies must match,
and the *Law of Attraction*
agrees with you.

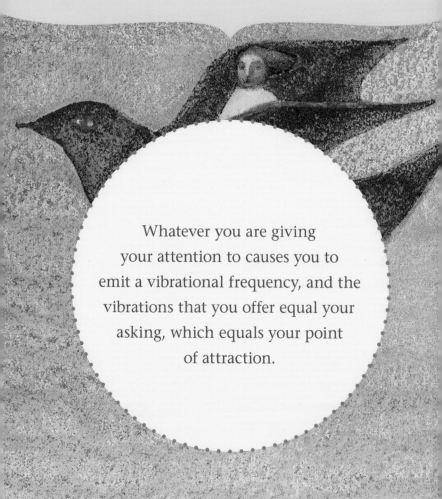

Whatever you are giving
your attention to causes you to
emit a vibrational frequency, and the
vibrations that you offer equal your
asking, which equals your point
of attraction.

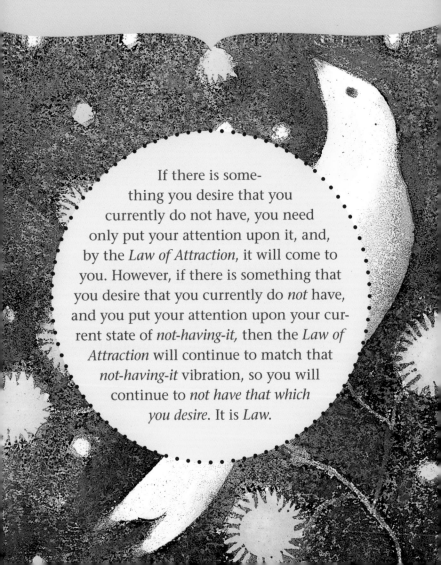

38

If there is some-
thing you desire that you
currently do not have, you need
only put your attention upon it, and,
by the *Law of Attraction*, it will come to
you. However, if there is something that
you desire that you currently do *not* have,
and you put your attention upon your current state of *not-having-it,* then the *Law of
Attraction* will continue to match that
not-having-it vibration, so you will
continue to *not have that which
you desire*. It is *Law.*

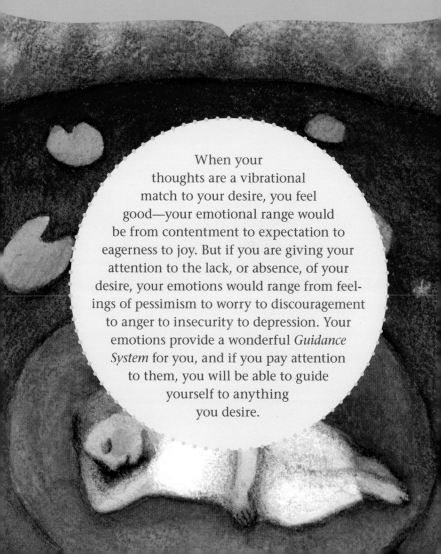

When your
thoughts are a vibrational
match to your desire, you feel
good—your emotional range would
be from contentment to expectation to
eagerness to joy. But if you are giving your
attention to the lack, or absence, of your
desire, your emotions would range from feelings of pessimism to worry to discouragement
to anger to insecurity to depression. Your
emotions provide a wonderful *Guidance
System* for you, and if you pay attention
to them, you will be able to guide
yourself to anything
you desire.

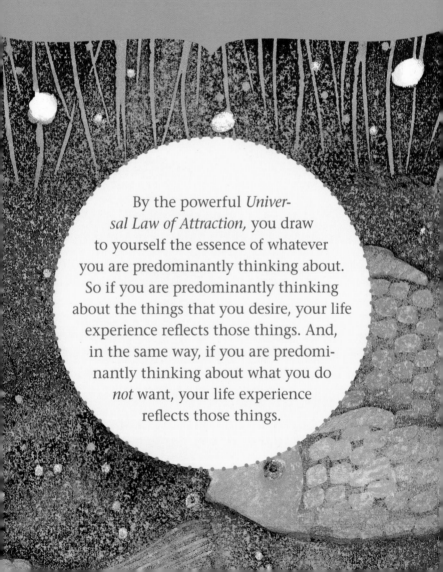

40

By the powerful *Univer-
sal Law of Attraction*, you draw
to yourself the essence of whatever
you are predominantly thinking about.
So if you are predominantly thinking
about the things that you desire, your life
experience reflects those things. And,
in the same way, if you are predominantly thinking about what you do
not want, your life experience
reflects those things.

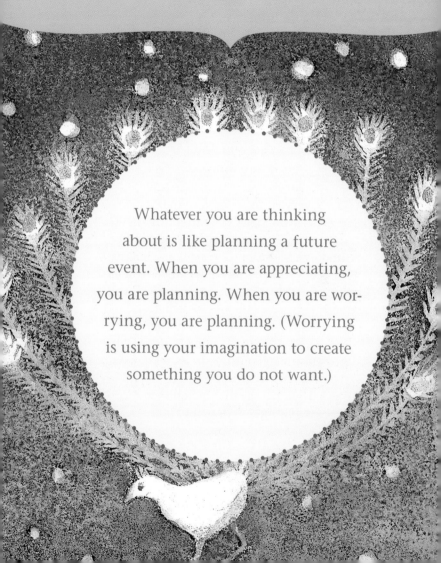

Whatever you are thinking about is like planning a future event. When you are appreciating, you are planning. When you are worrying, you are planning. (Worrying is using your imagination to create something you do not want.)

Every thought,
every idea, every Being,
every thing, is vibrational, so
when you focus your attention on
something, even for a short period of
time, the vibration of your Being begins
to reflect the vibration of whatever you are
giving your attention to. The more you think
about it, the more you vibrate like it; the more
you vibrate like it, the more of that which
is like it is attracted to you. That trend in
attraction will continue to increase until
a different vibration is offered—and
then things that match *that*
vibration are drawn to you,
by you.

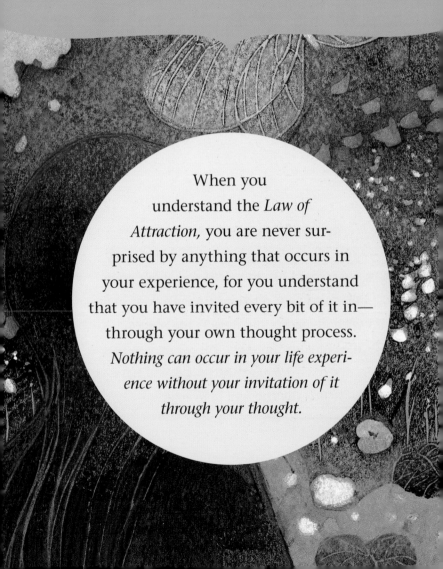

43

When you understand the *Law of Attraction*, you are never surprised by anything that occurs in your experience, for you understand that you have invited every bit of it in— through your own thought process. *Nothing can occur in your life experience without your invitation of it through your thought.*

There is a very
big vibrational difference
in your thoughts of *appreciation* of
your mate, and in your thoughts of what
you would like to be *different* about your
mate. And your relationship with your mate,
without exception, reflects the preponder-
ance of your thoughts. For, while you may
not have done it consciously, you have
literally thought your relationship into being.

45

Your desire for an improved financial condition cannot come to you if you often feel jealous of your neighbor's good fortune, for the vibration of your desire and the vibration of your jealous feelings are different vibrations. An understanding of your vibrational nature will make it possible for you to easily and deliberately create your own reality. And then, in time and with practice, you will discover that all desires that you hold can be easily realized—for there is nothing that you cannot be, do, or have.

You are Con-
sciousness. You are Energy.
You are Vibration. You are Elec-
tricity. You are Source Energy. You are
Creator. You are on the Leading Edge of
thought, and *even though it may seem odd to*
you at first, it will be helpful for you to begin
to accept yourself as a Vibrational Being, for
this is a Vibrational Universe in which you
are living, and the Laws that govern
this Universe are Vibrationally
based.

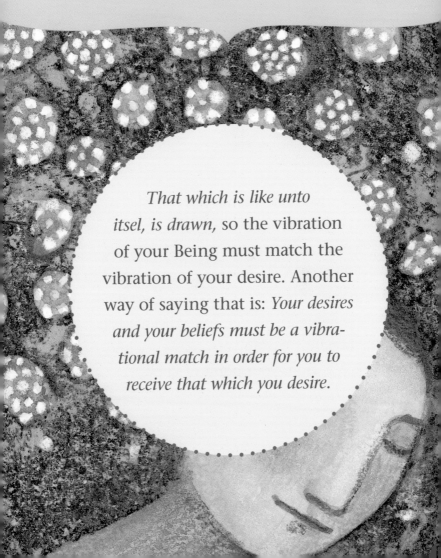

*That which is like unto
itsel, is drawn,* so the vibration
of your Being must match the
vibration of your desire. Another
way of saying that is: *Your desires
and your beliefs must be a vibrational match in order for you to
receive that which you desire.*

48

No matter what has caused
your unique point of view to
come about—it *has* come about. You
do exist; you are thinking; you are
perceiving; you are asking—and you
are being answered. And All-That-Is is
benefiting from your existence and
from your point of view.

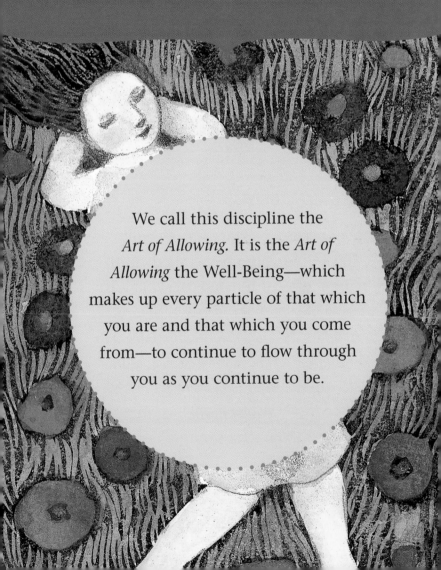

49

We call this discipline the *Art of Allowing.* It is the *Art of Allowing* the Well-Being—which makes up every particle of that which you are and that which you come from—to continue to flow through you as you continue to be.

50

Just as all of *your* experience, from the time of your birth into your physical body until now, has culminated into who *you* now are, *all that has ever been experienced by All-That-Is has culminated into all that is now being experienced in the physical life experience on planet Earth.*

If your involve-
ment in your time-space
reality inspires within you any
sincere desire, then the Universe has
the means to supply the results that you
seek. . . . The Stream of Well-Being flows
even if you do not understand that it does;
but when you *consciously* become aligned
with it, your creative endeavors become
so much more satisfying—for then you
discover that there is absolutely
nothing that you desire that
you cannot achieve.

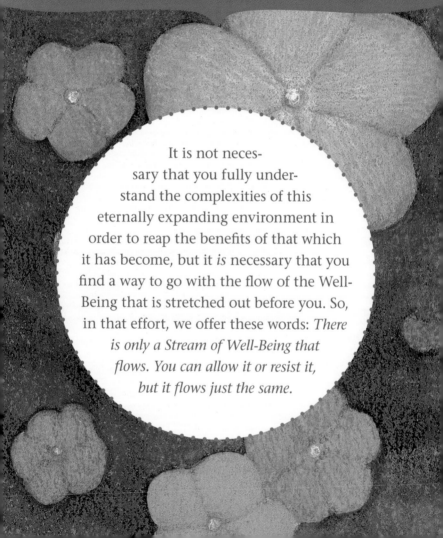

52

It is not neces-
sary that you fully understand the complexities of this
eternally expanding environment in
order to reap the benefits of that which
it has become, but it *is* necessary that you
find a way to go with the flow of the Well-
Being that is stretched out before you. So,
in that effort, we offer these words: *There
is only a Stream of Well-Being that
flows. You can allow it or resist it,
but it flows just the same.*

You would not
enter a brightly lit room
and look for the "dark switch."
You would not expect to find a
switch that would flood an inky darkness into the room to cover the brightness
of the light—you would find a switch that
would resist the light, for in the absence of
light there is darkness. And, in like manner,
there is not a Source of "evil," but there
could be a resisting of that which you
believe is Good, just as there is not a
Source of sickness, but there could
be a resisting of the natural
Well-Being.

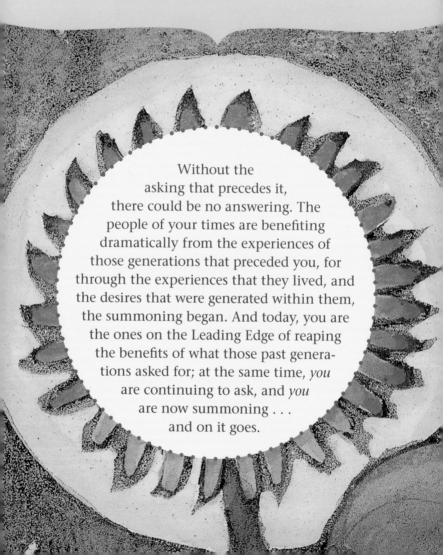

Without the
asking that precedes it,
there could be no answering. The
people of your times are benefiting
dramatically from the experiences of
those generations that preceded you, for
through the experiences that they lived, and
the desires that were generated within them,
the summoning began. And today, you are
the ones on the Leading Edge of reaping
the benefits of what those past generations asked for; at the same time, *you*
are continuing to ask, and *you*
are now summoning . . .
and on it goes.

There are some
people experiencing intense
hardships or traumas; and because of how they are living right now,
their *asking* is in a heightened and intense
place. And because of the intensity of their
requests, Source is responding in kind. And
although those who are doing the asking are
usually so involved in the trauma that they are
not personally receiving the benefit of their
own *asking,* future generations—or even
current generations who are not, right
now, disallowing—are receiving
the benefit of that *asking.*

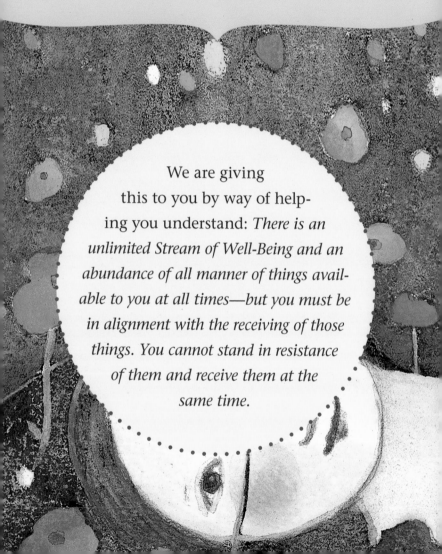

56

We are giving
this to you by way of helping you understand: *There is an
unlimited Stream of Well-Being and an
abundance of all manner of things available to you at all times—but you must be
in alignment with the receiving of those
things. You cannot stand in resistance
of them and receive them at the
same time.*

See yourself,
right where you are now,
as the beneficiary of the powerful Stream of Well-Being. Try to
imagine that you are basking in the
flow of this powerful Stream. Make an
effort to feel yourself as the Leading-
Edge beneficiary of this unlimited
Stream, and smile and try to
accept that you are
worthy of it.

58

You (and how you
feel) are all that is respon-
sible for whether you let in your
inheritance of Well-Being or not. And
while those around you may influence
you, more or less, to allow or not allow that
Stream, it is ultimately all up to you. You can
open the floodgates and let in your Well-
Being, or you can choose thoughts that keep
you pinched off from what is yours—but
whether you allow it or resist it, the Stream
is constantly flowing to you, never ending, never tiring, and always there
for your reconsideration.

Nothing has to change
in your environment or in the
circumstances that surround you for
you to begin to deliberately
allow your own connection to
the Stream of Well-Being. . . .
You are in the perfect place, right
now, to begin.

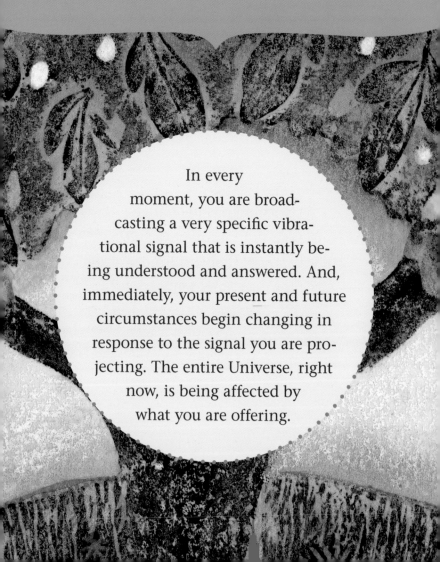

In every
moment, you are broad-
casting a very specific vibrational signal that is instantly being understood and answered. And,
immediately, your present and future
circumstances begin changing in
response to the signal you are projecting. The entire Universe, right
now, is being affected by
what you are offering.

Your world, present and future, is directly and specifically affected by the signal that you are now transmitting. The personality that is You is really an Eternal personality, but who you are right now, and what you are thinking right now, is causing a focusing of Energy that is very powerful. This Energy that you are focusing is the same Energy that creates worlds. And it is, in this very moment, creating your world.

Your feelings are the representatives of your *Guidance System*. In other words, the way you feel is your true indicator of your alignment with your Source, and of your alignment with your own intentions—both prebirth and currently.

Every thought
that has ever been thought
still exists; and whenever you focus
upon a thought, you activate the vibration of that thought within you. So, whatever you are currently giving your attention
to is an activated thought. But when you turn
your attention away from a thought, it becomes
dormant, or no longer active. As you give more
and more attention to any thought, and as you
focus upon it and therefore practice the
vibration of it, the thought becomes an
even bigger part of your vibration—
and you could now call this practiced thought a *belief.*

64

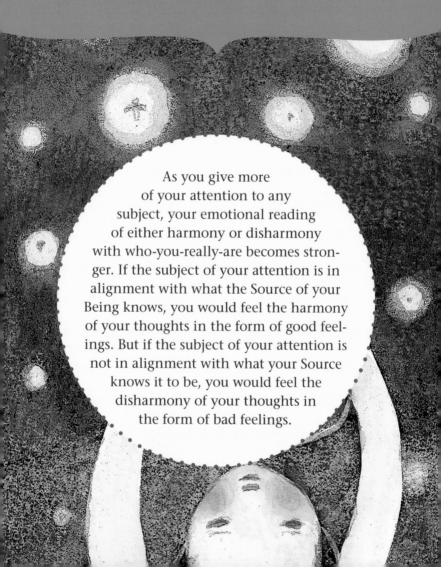

As you give more
of your attention to any
subject, your emotional reading
of either harmony or disharmony
with who-you-really-are becomes stronger. If the subject of your attention is in
alignment with what the Source of your
Being knows, you would feel the harmony
of your thoughts in the form of good feelings. But if the subject of your attention is
not in alignment with what your Source
knows it to be, you would feel the
disharmony of your thoughts in
the form of bad feelings.

Every thought
that you give your atten-
tion to expands and becomes a
bigger part of your vibrational mix.
Whether it is a thought of something
you want or a thought of something
you do not want, your attention to
it invites the essence of
the thought into your
experience.

Those who are mostly observers thrive in good times but suffer in bad times because what they are observing is already vibrating, and as they observe it, they include it in their vibrational countenance; and as they include it, the Universe accepts that as their point of attraction—and gives them more of the essence of it. So, for an observer, the better it gets, the better it gets; or the worse it gets, the worse it gets. However, one who is a visionary thrives in *all* times.

With your practiced attention to any subject, the *Law of Attraction* delivers circumstances, conditions, experiences, other people, and all manner of things that match your habitual dominant vibration. And as things begin to manifest around you that match the thoughts you have been holding, you now develop stronger and stronger vibrational habits or proclivities. And so, your once-small and insignificant thought has now evolved into a powerful belief—and your powerful beliefs will always be played out in your experience.

Your sense of
taste or smell or hearing
or sight is not usually the way
you recognize a hot stove, but as you
approach the stove with your body, the
sensors in your skin let you know if the
stove is hot. And in the same way that you
utilize your sensitive, sophisticated transla-
tors of vibration (your five physical senses)
to interpret your physical life experience,
you were also born with other sensors—
your emotions—that are additional
vibrational interpreters that help you
understand, in the moment, the
experiences that you
are living.

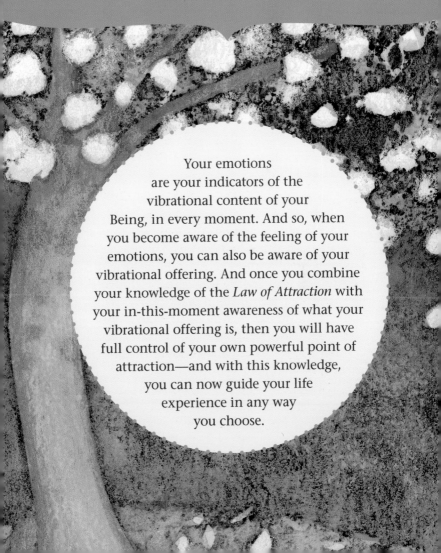

Your emotions
are your indicators of the
vibrational content of your
Being, in every moment. And so, when
you become aware of the feeling of your
emotions, you can also be aware of your
vibrational offering. And once you combine
your knowledge of the *Law of Attraction* with
your in-this-moment awareness of what your
vibrational offering is, then you will have
full control of your own powerful point of
attraction—and with this knowledge,
you can now guide your life
experience in any way
you choose.

Your emotions indicate the degree of your alignment with Source, and although you can never disconnect from it altogether, the thoughts you choose to give your attention to *do* give you a substantial range in alignment or misalignment with the Non-Physical Energy that is truly who-you-are. And so, with time and practice, you will come to know, in every moment, your degree of alignment with who-you-really-are, for when you are in full allowance of the Energy of your Source, you thrive; and to the degree that you do not allow this alignment, you do not thrive.

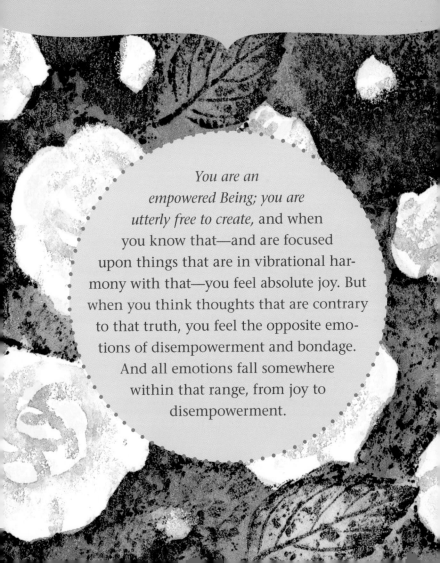

You are an empowered Being; you are utterly free to create, and when you know that—and are focused upon things that are in vibrational harmony with that—you feel absolute joy. But when you think thoughts that are contrary to that truth, you feel the opposite emotions of disempowerment and bondage. And all emotions fall somewhere within that range, from joy to disempowerment.

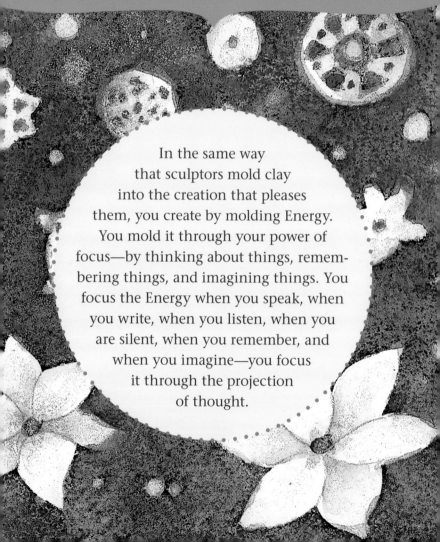

In the same way
that sculptors mold clay
into the creation that pleases
them, you create by molding Energy.
You mold it through your power of
focus—by thinking about things, remembering things, and imagining things. You
focus the Energy when you speak, when
you write, when you listen, when you
are silent, when you remember, and
when you imagine—you focus
it through the projection
of thought.

All things that
you ask for, large and small,
are immediately understood and
fully offered, without exception.
Every point of Consciousness has the
right and the ability to ask, and all points of
Consciousness are honored and responded to
immediately. When you ask, it is given—every
time! Your "asking" is sometimes spoken with
your words, but more often it emanates from
you vibrationally as a constant stream of
personally honed preferences, each
building on the next, and each
one respected and answered.

Every subject is really two subjects: There is that which you desire, and the lack of it. Often— even when you believe you are thinking about something that you desire— you are actually thinking about the exact opposite of what you desire.

What you think and what you get is always a perfect vibrational match, so it can be very helpful to make a conscious correlation between what you are thinking and what is manifesting in your life experience, but it is even more helpful if you are able to discern where you are headed even before you get there. Once you understand your emotions and what your vibrational offering has been, you can tell, by the way you feel, exactly where you are headed.

You are not
always aware that your
desires have been answered
because there is often a time gap
between your *asking* and your *allowing*.
Even though a clear desire has emanated as
a result of the contrast you have considered,
you often, rather than giving your attention
purely to the desire itself, focus back on the
contrasting situation that gave birth to the
desire—and in doing so, your vibration
is more about the reason why you
have launched the desire rather
than the desire itself.

With each
statement of need and
justification, you unwittingly
reinforce the vibration of your current unpleasant situation, and in doing
so, you continue to hold yourself out
of vibrational alignment with your new
desire and out of the receiving mode of
what you are asking for. . . . *As long as
you are more aware of what you <u>do not</u>
want regarding a situation, what you
<u>do</u> want cannot come
to you.*

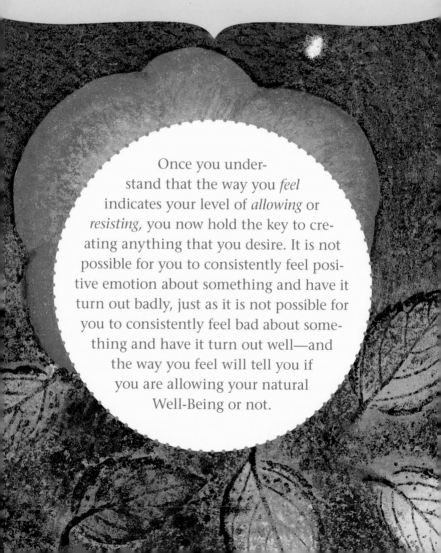

78

Once you under-
stand that the way you *feel*
indicates your level of *allowing* or
resisting, you now hold the key to creating anything that you desire. It is not
possible for you to consistently feel positive emotion about something and have it
turn out badly, just as it is not possible for
you to consistently feel bad about something and have it turn out well—and
the way you feel will tell you if
you are allowing your natural
Well-Being or not.

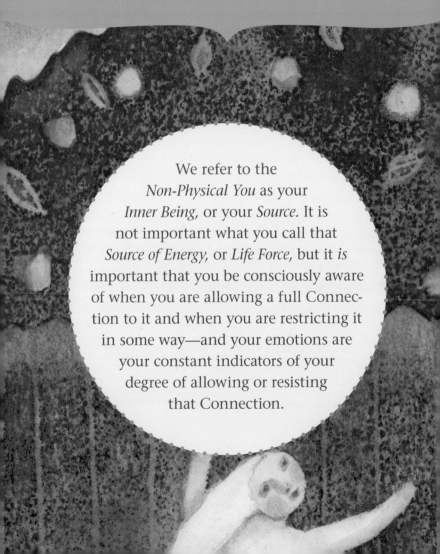

We refer to the
Non-Physical You as your
Inner Being, or your *Source.* It is
not important what you call that
Source of Energy, or *Life Force,* but it *is*
important that you be consciously aware
of when you are allowing a full Connection to it and when you are restricting it
in some way—and your emotions are
your constant indicators of your
degree of allowing or resisting
that Connection.

As you con-
sciously consider the way
you feel, you will get better
and better at directing the Source
Energy, and you will become a dis-
ciplined and joyous *Deliberate Creator*.
With practice, you will be able to achieve
focused control of this *Creative Energy;*
and, like the skilled sculptor, you will
take delight in the molding of this
Energy that creates worlds, and
direct it toward your individ-
ual creative endeavors.

When you are
thinking about something
that you have been wanting for a
very long time—and you are noticing
that it has not yet happened—a strong
negative emotion would be present within
you. However, if you are thinking about
something that you have been wanting—and
you are imagining that it *is* happening—
then your emotion would be one of anticipation or eagerness. And so, you can tell
by the way you *feel* whether you are,
in this moment, allowing or
resisting your desire.

We are not
encouraging you to make
an effort to *control* your thoughts,
but instead, to make an effort to
more or less *guide* your thoughts. And it
is not even so much about guiding your
thoughts as it is about reaching for a *feeling,* because reaching for the way you
would like to *feel* is an easier way to
hold your thoughts in vibrational
alignment with that which you
believe is good.

Whenever you have con-
sistently focused upon a subject,
causing a consistent vibrational activa-
tion of it within you, it becomes a practiced or dominant thought. *And once your
focused attention has sufficiently activated
a dominant vibration within you, things—
wanted or unwanted—will begin to make
their way into your personal experience. It is <u>Law.</u>*

84

Before you can
effectively benefit from
paying attention to your emotions, you must first accept that
Well-Being is the only Stream that flows.
You can allow or disallow this Stream,
but when you allow it, you feel well; and
when you disallow it, you feel sick. In
other words, there is only a Stream of
wellness, which you are allowing or
resisting, and you can tell by the
way you *feel* which you
are doing.

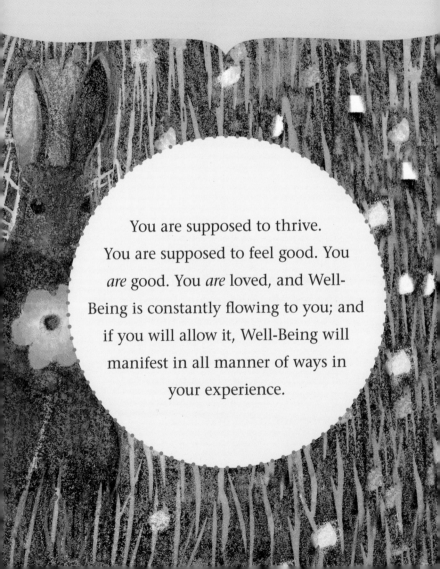

85

You are supposed to thrive.
You are supposed to feel good. You
are good. You *are* loved, and Well-
Being is constantly flowing to you; and
if you will allow it, Well-Being will
manifest in all manner of ways in
your experience.

A *belief* is only a
practiced vibration. In other
words, once you have practiced a
thought long enough, then, anytime
you approach the subject of that thought,
the *Law of Attraction* will take you easily
into the full vibration of your belief. And so,
as you have a life experience that matches
those thoughts you were pondering, you
conclude, "Yes, this is truth." And while
it may be accurate to call it "truth,"
we would prefer to call it
attraction or *creation*.

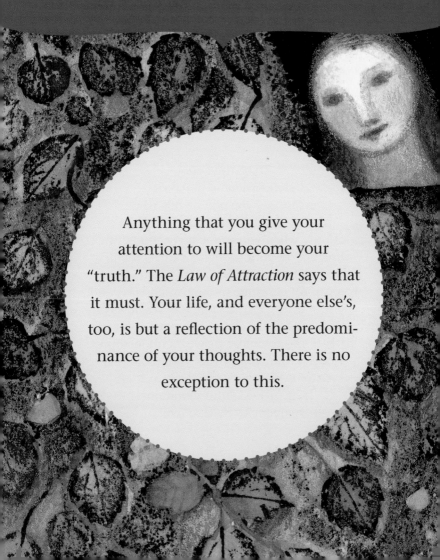

Anything that you give your attention to will become your "truth." The *Law of Attraction* says that it must. Your life, and everyone else's, too, is but a reflection of the predominance of your thoughts. There is no exception to this.

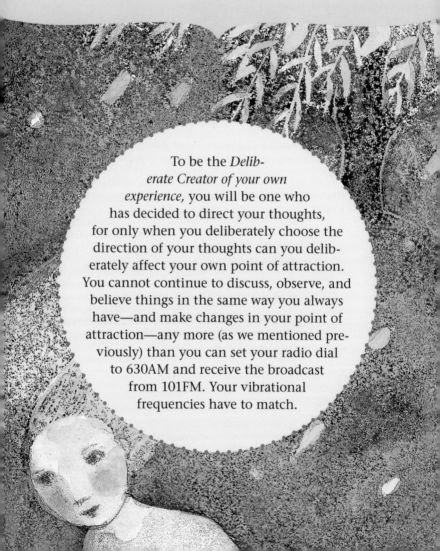

To be the *Delib-
erate Creator of your own
experience,* you will be one who
has decided to direct your thoughts,
for only when you deliberately choose the
direction of your thoughts can you deliberately affect your own point of attraction.
You cannot continue to discuss, observe, and
believe things in the same way you always
have—and make changes in your point of
attraction—any more (as we mentioned pre-
viously) than you can set your radio dial
to 630AM and receive the broadcast
from 101FM. Your vibrational
frequencies have to match.

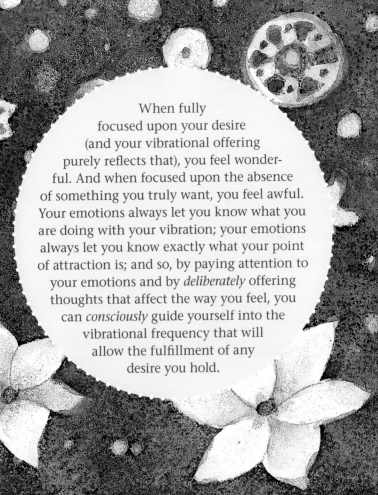

When fully
focused upon your desire
(and your vibrational offering
purely reflects that), you feel wonderful. And when focused upon the absence
of something you truly want, you feel awful.
Your emotions always let you know what you
are doing with your vibration; your emotions
always let you know exactly what your point
of attraction is; and so, by paying attention to
your emotions and by *deliberately* offering
thoughts that affect the way you feel, you
can *consciously* guide yourself into the
vibrational frequency that will
allow the fulfillment of any
desire you hold.

Once you
begin to accept yourself
as a Vibrational Being who attracts all things that come into your
experience, and once you understand
the correlation between what you are
thinking and feeling and what you are
receiving—then you hold the keys to
get from wherever you are to wherever you want to be, on all
subjects.

Most people do not believe that they have control over what they believe. They observe things happening around them and evaluate them, but they usually feel that they have no control whatsoever about the belief that is formulating within them. They spend their lives sorting events into categories of good or bad, wanted or unwanted, right or wrong—but rarely do they understand that they have the ability to control their personal relationship with these events.

Through personal
force, or gathering in groups
to gain the feeling of more power,
many people seek to preserve their own
Well-Being by attempting to take control
of any circumstances that they believe could
threaten it. But in this attraction-based Universe where there is no such thing as exclusion,
the harder they push against unwanted things,
the more they achieve vibrational alignment
with unwanted things—and, in doing so, the
more they invite unwanted things into their
own experience. . . . The more you
defend your own beliefs, the more
the *Law of Attraction* helps you
live them out.

With enough attention to anything, the essence of what you have been giving thought to will eventually become a physical manifestation. And then as others observe your physical manifestation, through their attention to it they help it to expand. And then, in time, this manifestation, whether it is one that is wanted or not, is called "Truth." Deliberate Creation is about deliberately choosing those experiences you make your Truths.

When your newly
activated thoughts are gen-
eral and not very focused, those
vibrations are still very small and
do not yet have much attraction power;
and so, in these early stages, you would not
likely see any manifested evidence of your
attention to the subject. But as the thought
gains momentum, you now begin to get an
emotional reading on how well this growing
thought-vibration is matching the Energy
of your Source. If it matches who-you-are,
your good-feeling emotions indicate
that. If it does *not* match who-you-
are, your bad-feeling emotions indicate that.

When you
continue to focus upon
any thought, it becomes increas-
ingly easy to continue to focus upon
it because the *Law of Attraction* is making more thoughts like it available to you.
Emotionally speaking, you are developing
a mood or an attitude. Vibrationally
speaking, you are achieving a habitual vibrational groove, so to
speak—or a *set-point*.

Your *emotional
set-points* can change from
not feeling good to feeling good,
for your *set-points* are achieved simply by paying attention to a subject
and through your practiced thought. And
we want you to understand the extreme
value in deliberately achieving your own
set-points, because, once you expect something, it will come. The details of it
may play out differently, but the
vibrational essence will always
be an exact match.

Every living
thing—animal, human, or
plant—experiences that which is
called *death,* with no exception. Spirit,
which is who-we-really-are, is Eternal. So
what death must be is but a changing of
the perspective of that Eternal Spirit. If you
are standing in your physical body and consciously connected to that Spirit, then you
are Eternal in nature and you need never
fear any "endedness," because, from that
perspective, there is none. (You will
never cease to be, for you are
Eternal Consciousness.)

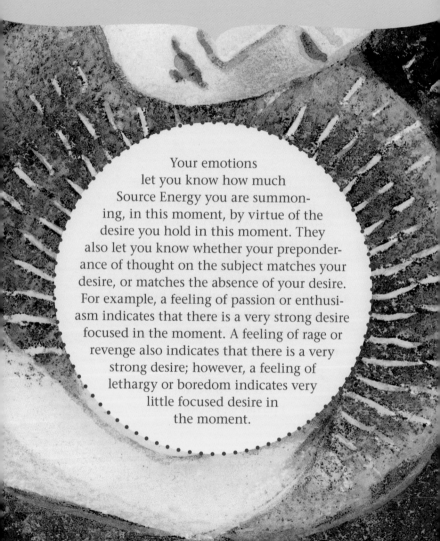

Your emotions
let you know how much
Source Energy you are summoning, in this moment, by virtue of the
desire you hold in this moment. They
also let you know whether your preponder-
ance of thought on the subject matches your
desire, or matches the absence of your desire.
For example, a feeling of passion or enthusiasm indicates that there is a very strong desire
focused in the moment. A feeling of rage or
revenge also indicates that there is a very
strong desire; however, a feeling of
lethargy or boredom indicates very
little focused desire in
the moment.

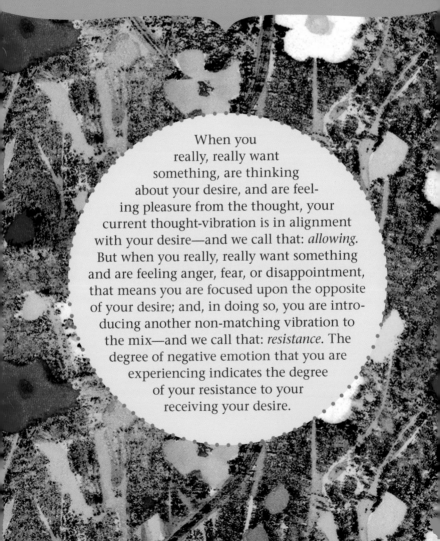

When you
really, really want
something, are thinking
about your desire, and are feeling pleasure from the thought, your
current thought-vibration is in alignment
with your desire—and we call that: *allowing.*
But when you really, really want something
and are feeling anger, fear, or disappointment,
that means you are focused upon the opposite
of your desire; and, in doing so, you are intro-
ducing another non-matching vibration to
the mix—and we call that: *resistance.* The
degree of negative emotion that you are
experiencing indicates the degree
of your resistance to your
receiving your desire.

100

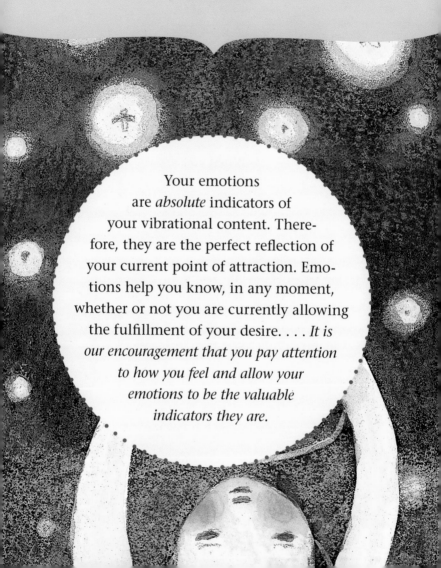

Your emotions
are *absolute* indicators of
your vibrational content. Therefore, they are the perfect reflection of
your current point of attraction. Emotions help you know, in any moment,
whether or not you are currently allowing
the fulfillment of your desire. . . . *It is
our encouragement that you pay attention
to how you feel and allow your
emotions to be the valuable
indicators they are.*

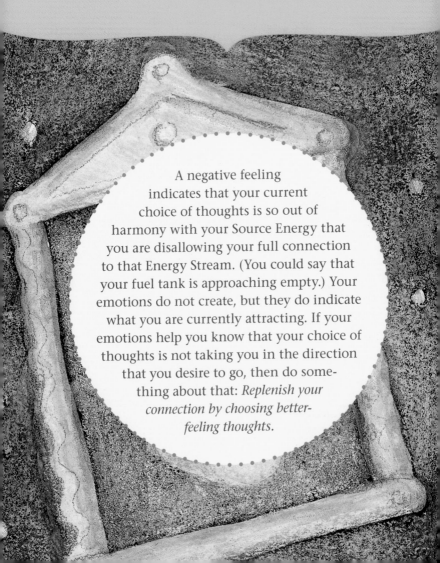

A negative feeling indicates that your current choice of thoughts is so out of harmony with your Source Energy that you are disallowing your full connection to that Energy Stream. (You could say that your fuel tank is approaching empty.) Your emotions do not create, but they do indicate what you are currently attracting. If your emotions help you know that your choice of thoughts is not taking you in the direction that you desire to go, then do something about that: *Replenish your connection by choosing better-feeling thoughts.*

102

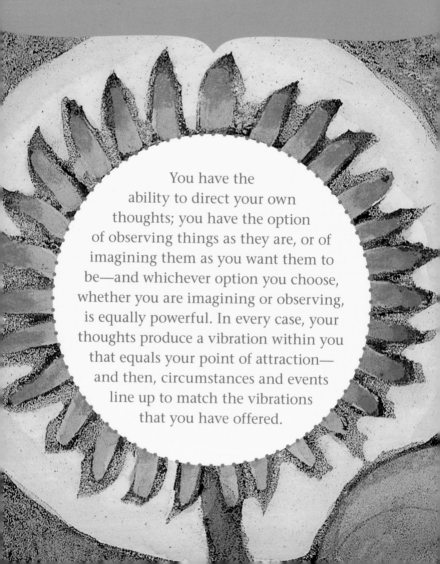

You have the
ability to direct your own
thoughts; you have the option
of observing things as they are, or of
imagining them as you want them to
be—and whichever option you choose,
whether you are imagining or observing,
is equally powerful. In every case, your
thoughts produce a vibration within you
that equals your point of attraction—
and then, circumstances and events
line up to match the vibrations
that you have offered.

When you find yourself engulfed in circumstances that cause you to offer a vibration that is far from that of bliss, then instantly reaching bliss is an impossible thing, for the *Law of Attraction* does not allow you to make that vibrational jump any more than you could have tuned your radio receiver to 101FM and heard a song that was being played on 630AM.

It is not a dif-
ficult thing to change the
pattern of your vibration, espe-
cially when you understand that you
can do it a little bit at a time. Once you
have an understanding of how vibrations
work, how they affect your experience,
and, most important, what your emotions
are telling you about your vibrations,
now you can make steady, fast prog-
ress toward the achievement of
anything that you desire.

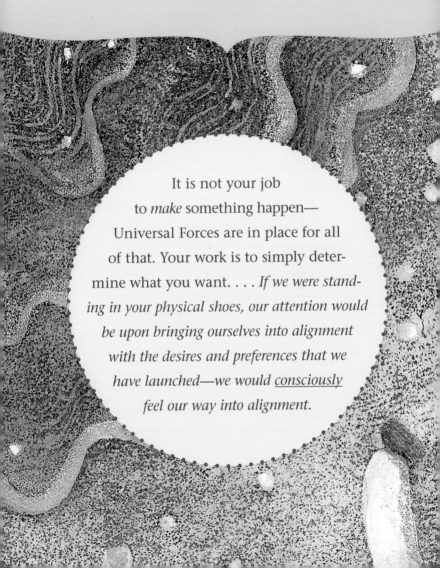

It is not your job
to *make* something happen—
Universal Forces are in place for all
of that. Your work is to simply determine what you want. . . . *If we were standing in your physical shoes, our attention would
be upon bringing ourselves into alignment
with the desires and preferences that we
have launched—we would <u>consciously</u>
feel our way into alignment.*

All of your desires, wants, or preferences emanate from you naturally and constantly, for you stand at the Leading Edge of a Universe that makes that so. So, you cannot hold your desires back; the Eternal nature of this Universe insists that your desires come forth.

Regarding your creation of your own life experience, *there really is only one important question for you to ask:* "How can I bring myself into vibrational alignment with the desires that my experience has produced?" *And the answer is simple:* Pay attention to the way you feel, and deliberately choose thoughts—about everything—that feel good to you when you think them.

108

As you made the
decision to come into this
body, you knew that you were
a creator and that the Earth environment would inspire your specific creation. You also knew that whenever you
asked, it would be given. And you were
thrilled by the prospect of being inspired
to attain your own specific desires,
understanding that Source would
flow through you to achieve
the completion of those
desires.

We refer to the time between your offering of a thought and its physical manifestation as "the buffer of time." It is that wonderful time of offering thought . . . noticing how it feels . . . adjusting the thought to achieve an even better feeling . . . and then, in an attitude of absolute expectation, enjoying the gentle, steady unfolding of anything and everything that you have concluded as your desires.

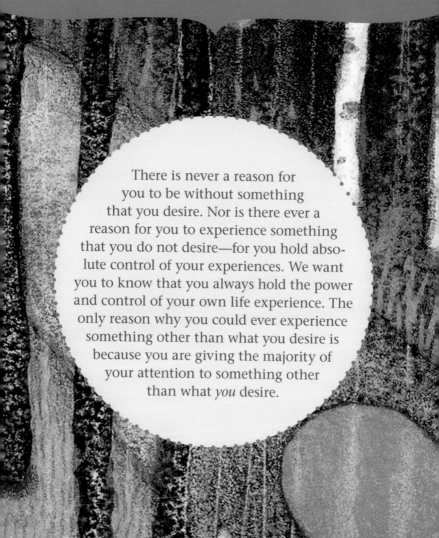

110

There is never a reason for you to be without something that you desire. Nor is there ever a reason for you to experience something that you do not desire—for you hold absolute control of your experiences. We want you to know that you always hold the power and control of your own life experience. The only reason why you could ever experience something other than what you desire is because you are giving the majority of your attention to something other than what *you* desire.

The *Law of Attraction* always yields to you the essence of the balance of your thoughts. No exceptions. You get what you think about—whether you want it or not. And, in time, and with practice, you will come to remember that the *Law of Attraction* is always consistent. It never tricks you; it never deceives you; it never confuses you, for the *Law of Attraction* responds precisely to the vibration that you are offering.

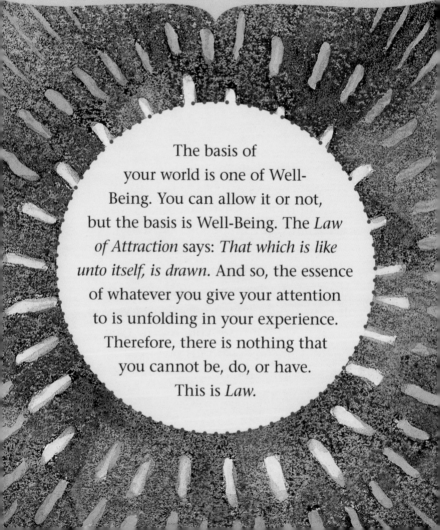

The basis of
your world is one of Well-
Being. You can allow it or not,
but the basis is Well-Being. The *Law
of Attraction* says: *That which is like
unto itself, is drawn.* And so, the essence
of whatever you give your attention
to is unfolding in your experience.
Therefore, there is nothing that
you cannot be, do, or have.
This is *Law.*

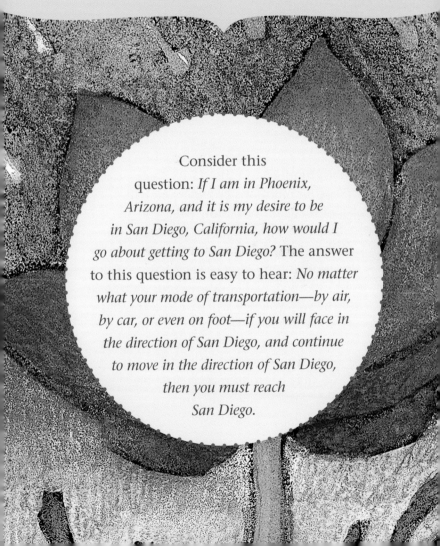

Consider this question: *If I am in Phoenix, Arizona, and it is my desire to be in San Diego, California, how would I go about getting to San Diego?* The answer to this question is easy to hear: *No matter what your mode of transportation—by air, by car, or even on foot—if you will face in the direction of San Diego, and continue to move in the direction of San Diego, then you must reach San Diego.*

114

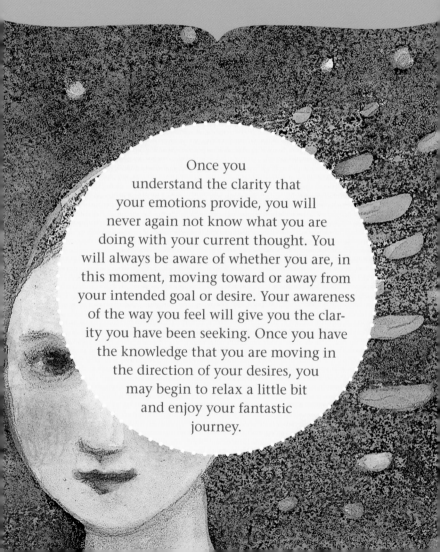

Once you
understand the clarity that
your emotions provide, you will
never again not know what you are
doing with your current thought. You
will always be aware of whether you are, in
this moment, moving toward or away from
your intended goal or desire. Your awareness
of the way you feel will give you the clarity you have been seeking. Once you have
the knowledge that you are moving in
the direction of your desires, you
may begin to relax a little bit
and enjoy your fantastic
journey.

You are a perfect yet expanding Being, in a perfect yet expanding world. Your expansion is a given, the expansion of your time-space reality is a given, and the expansion of this Universe is a given—it is just ever so much more satisfying for you to consciously and deliberately participate in your own expansion.

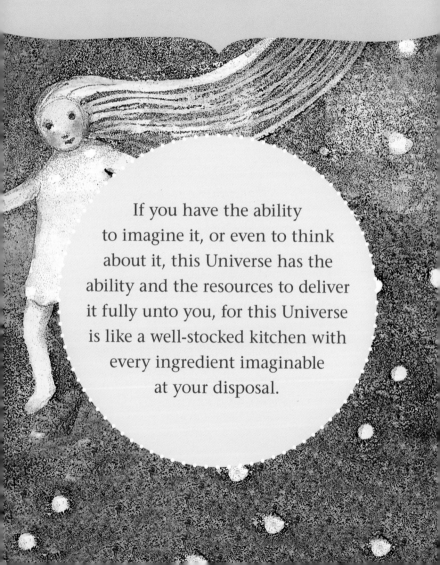

If you have the ability
to imagine it, or even to think
about it, this Universe has the
ability and the resources to deliver
it fully unto you, for this Universe
is like a well-stocked kitchen with
every ingredient imaginable
at your disposal.

Without the abil-
ity to know what you do *not*
want, you could not know what
you *do* want. And so, it is through your
exposure to life experience that your natural preferences are born. In fact, these preferences are exuding from you in all moments
of every day, at many levels of your Being.
Even the cells of your well-tended-to body are
having their own experience and are ema-
nating *their* own preferences—and every
preference is recognized by Source and
immediately answered, with
no exceptions.

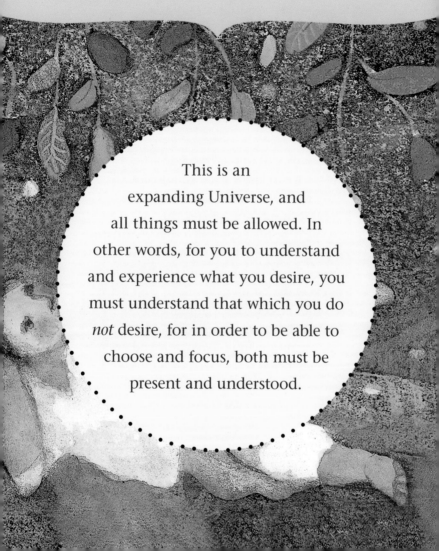

This is an expanding Universe, and all things must be allowed. In other words, for you to understand and experience what you desire, you must understand that which you do *not* desire, for in order to be able to choose and focus, both must be present and understood.

Every physical Being on your
Planet is your partner in
co-creation, and if you would accept
that and appreciate the diversity of
beliefs and desires—all of you would
have more expansive, satisfying,
and fulfilling experiences.

Imagine yourself as a chef in an extremely well-stocked kitchen that contains every imaginable ingredient, and as you proceed, there are many ingredients that are *not* appropriate for your creation, so you do not utilize them, but you also feel no discomfort about their existence. You simply utilize the ingredients that *will* enhance your creation— and you leave the ingredients that are not appropriate for your creation out of your pie.

From your Non-Physical perspective, you understood that there is room enough in this expansive Universe for all manner of thought and experience. You had every intention of being deliberate about your own creative control of your own life experience and your own creations—but you had no intention of trying to control the creations of others.

From the variety,
or contrast, your preferences
or desires are born. And in the
moment that your preference begins to
exist, it begins to draw to itself—through
the *Law of Attraction*—the essence of that
which matches it . . . and it then begins an
immediate expansion. This is how the Universe
expands, and this is why you are on the Leading
Edge of the expansion. The valuable contrast
continues to provide the birthing of endless
new desires, and as each desire is born,
Source responds to the desire—it is a
never-ending, always-flowing, pure,
positive Energy expansion.

You cannot
ever get it done because
you cannot ever cease to be,
and neither can you ever halt your
awareness. Yet, out of your awareness
will always be born another asking,
and each asking always summons
another answering. Your Eternal
nature is one of expansion—and in
that expansion is the potential
for unspeakable joy.

The contrast causes a new desire to be born within you; the new desire radiates from you, and as you offer the vibration of your new desire, that desire is answered—every time. When you ask, it is given. Now think about the perfection of this process: *Continuing new ideas for the improvement of your experience emanate from you constantly, and are answered constantly.* Feel the balance and perfection of your environment: *Every point of Consciousness, even the Consciousness of a cell in your body, can request an improved state of being—and get it.*

Each point of view matters;
every request is granted; and as this
amazing Universe unerringly expands,
there is no end to the Universal resources
that fulfill these requests. And there is no
end to the answers to the never-ending
stream of questions—and, for that
reason, there is no competition.

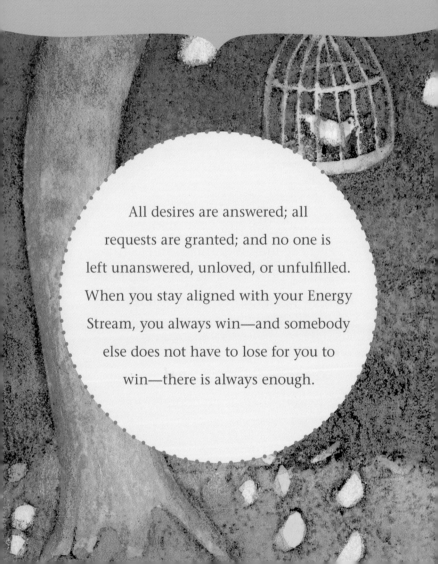

All desires are answered; all requests are granted; and no one is left unanswered, unloved, or unfulfilled. When you stay aligned with your Energy Stream, you always win—and somebody else does not have to lose for you to win—there is always enough.

If someone is
not receiving what they are
asking for, it is not because there
is a shortage of resources; it can only
be that the person holding the desire is
out of alignment with their own request.
There is no shortage; there is no lack;
there is no competition for resources—
there is only the allowing or the
disallowing of that which you
are asking for.

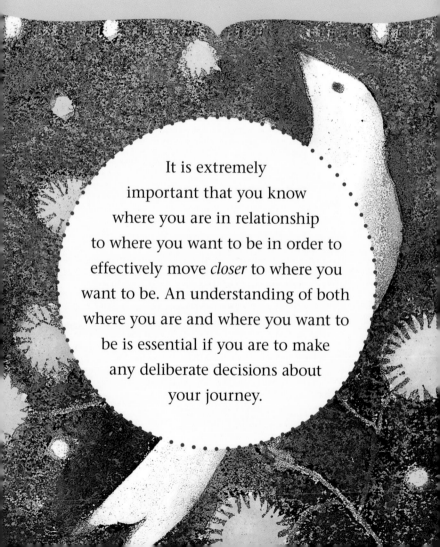

It is extremely important that you know where you are in relationship to where you want to be in order to effectively move *closer* to where you want to be. An understanding of both where you are and where you want to be is essential if you are to make any deliberate decisions about your journey.

129

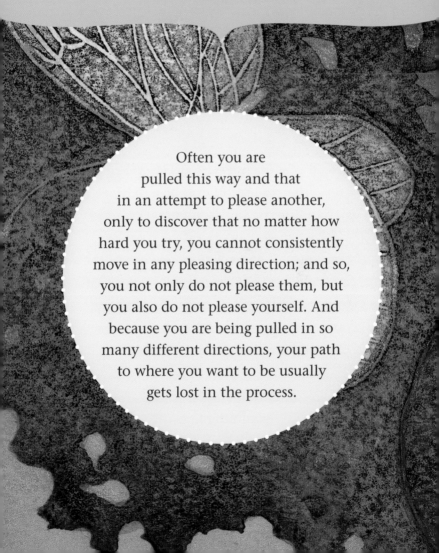

Often you are
pulled this way and that
in an attempt to please another,
only to discover that no matter how
hard you try, you cannot consistently
move in any pleasing direction; and so,
you not only do not please them, but
you also do not please yourself. And
because you are being pulled in so
many different directions, your path
to where you want to be usually
gets lost in the process.

The greatest gift
that you could ever give to
another is your own happiness,
for when you are in a state of joy or
happiness or appreciation, you are fully
connected to the Stream of pure, positive
Source Energy that is truly who-you-are.
And when you are in that state of connection, anything or anyone that you
are holding as your object of
attention benefits from
your attention.

Your
happiness does
not depend on what
others do, but only upon your
own vibrational balance. And the
happiness of others does not depend
on you, but only upon *their* own vibrational balance, for the way anyone feels,
in any moment, is only about their own
mix of Energies. The way you feel is simply, clearly, and always the indicator of
the vibrational balance between your
desires and your vibrational offering, which, from your vantage point, you have
launched.

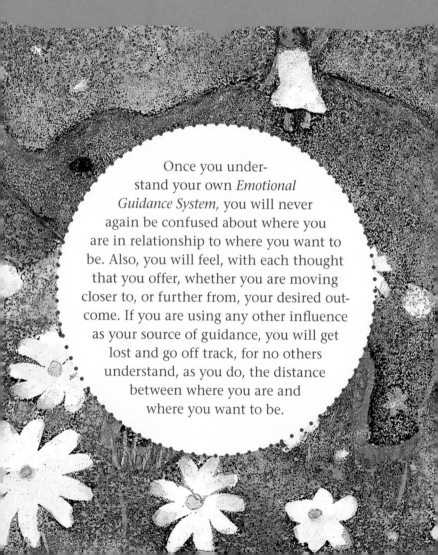

132

Once you under-
stand your own *Emotional
Guidance System*, you will never
again be confused about where you
are in relationship to where you want to
be. Also, you will feel, with each thought
that you offer, whether you are moving
closer to, or further from, your desired outcome. If you are using any other influence
as your source of guidance, you will get
lost and go off track, for no others
understand, as you do, the distance
between where you are and
where you want to be.

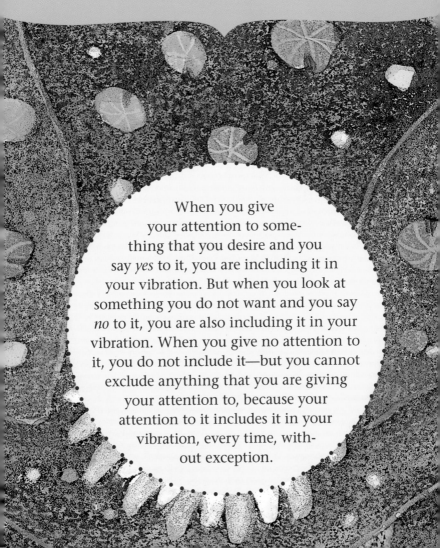

When you give
your attention to some-
thing that you desire and you
say *yes* to it, you are including it in
your vibration. But when you look at
something you do not want and you say
no to it, you are also including it in your
vibration. When you give no attention to
it, you do not include it—but you cannot
exclude anything that you are giving
your attention to, because your
attention to it includes it in your
vibration, every time, without exception.

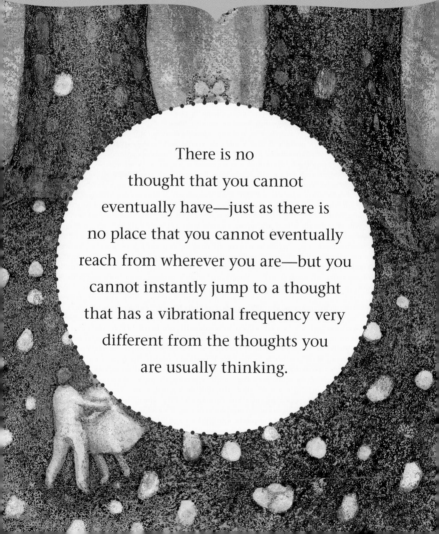

There is no
thought that you cannot
eventually have—just as there is
no place that you cannot eventually
reach from wherever you are—but you
cannot instantly jump to a thought
that has a vibrational frequency very
different from the thoughts you
are usually thinking.

Decide to *reach
for the best-feeling thought
that you have access to.* A good
way to feel your way up this
Vibrational Emotional Scale is to always
be reaching for the feeling of relief that
comes when you release a more resistant
thought and replace it with a more allowing thought. The Stream of Well-Being is
always flowing through you; and the
more you allow it, the better you
feel. The more you resist it,
the worse you feel.

There is no con-
dition so severe that you
cannot reverse it by choosing
different thoughts. However, choosing different thoughts requires focus
and practice. If you continue to focus
as you have been, to think as you have
been, and to believe as you have
been, then nothing in your
experience will change.

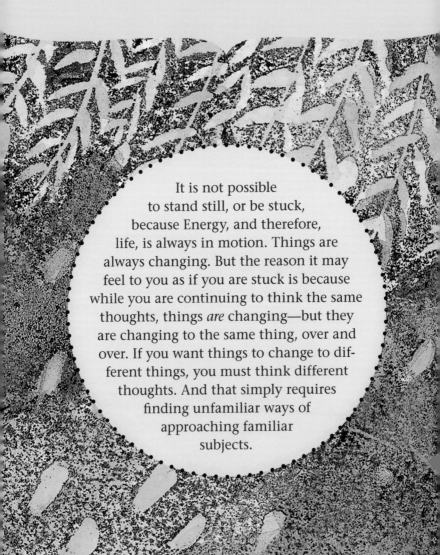

It is not possible
to stand still, or be stuck,
because Energy, and therefore,
life, is always in motion. Things are
always changing. But the reason it may
feel to you as if you are stuck is because
while you are continuing to think the same
thoughts, things *are* changing—but they
are changing to the same thing, over and
over. If you want things to change to different things, you must think different
thoughts. And that simply requires
finding unfamiliar ways of
approaching familiar
subjects.

Others cannot
understand the vibra-
tional content of your desires,
and they cannot understand the
vibrational content of where you are,
so they are not in any way equipped to
guide you. Even when they have the very
best of intentions and want your absolute Well-Being, they do not know. And
even though many of them attempt to
be unselfish, it is never possible for
them to separate their desire for
you from their own desire
for themselves.

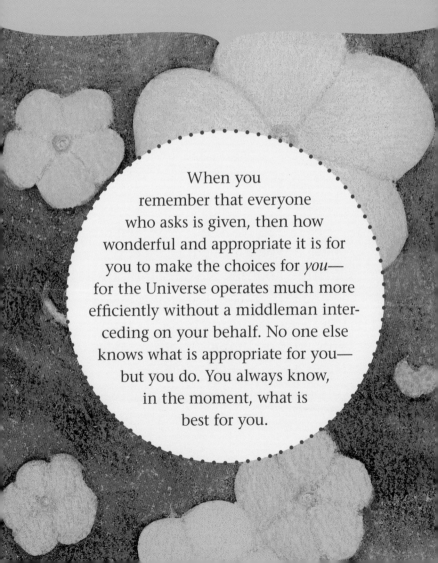

When you
remember that everyone
who asks is given, then how
wonderful and appropriate it is for
you to make the choices for *you*—
for the Universe operates much more
efficiently without a middleman inter-
ceding on your behalf. No one else
knows what is appropriate for you—
but you do. You always know,
in the moment, what is
best for you.

When you know
that you want something
and you notice that you do not
have it, you assume that there is
something outside of yourself that is
keeping it from you, but that is never
true. The only thing that ever pre-
vents your receiving something that
you desire is that your habit of
thought is different from
your desire.

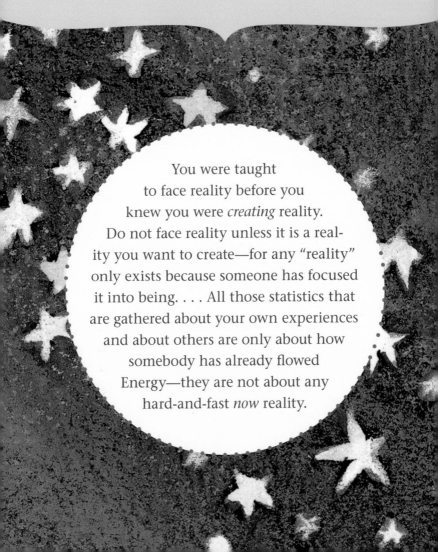

141

You were taught
to face reality before you
knew you were *creating* reality.
Do not face reality unless it is a reality you want to create—for any "reality"
only exists because someone has focused
it into being. . . . All those statistics that
are gathered about your own experiences
and about others are only about how
somebody has already flowed
Energy—they are not about any
hard-and-fast *now* reality.

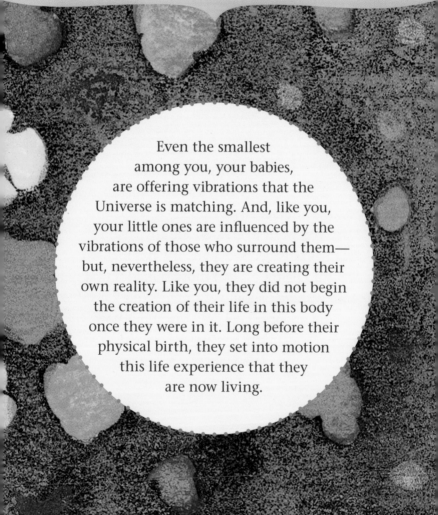

Even the smallest
among you, your babies,
are offering vibrations that the
Universe is matching. And, like you,
your little ones are influenced by the
vibrations of those who surround them—
but, nevertheless, they are creating their
own reality. Like you, they did not begin
the creation of their life in this body
once they were in it. Long before their
physical birth, they set into motion
this life experience that they
are now living.

If you were driv-
ing your vehicle at 100
miles per hour and you hit a tree,
you would experience a very big crash.
However, if you were to hit the same tree
while your vehicle was traveling at just 5
miles per hour, the outcome would be consid-
erably different. See the speed of your vehicle
like the power of your desire. In other words,
the more you want something, or the longer
you have been focusing upon your desire,
the faster the Energy moves. The tree in
our analogy represents the resistance,
or the contradictory thoughts,
that may be present.

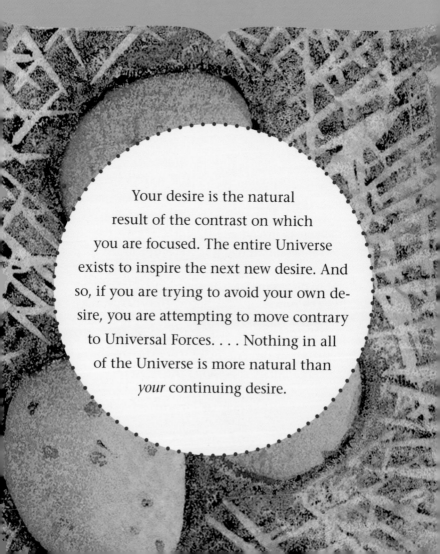

Your desire is the natural
result of the contrast on which
you are focused. The entire Universe
exists to inspire the next new desire. And
so, if you are trying to avoid your own desire, you are attempting to move contrary
to Universal Forces. . . . Nothing in all
of the Universe is more natural than
your continuing desire.

There is no desire that anyone holds for any other reason than that they believe they will feel better in the achievement of it. Whether it is a material object, a physical state of being, a relationship, a condition, or a circumstance—at the heart of every desire is the desire to feel good. And so, the standard of success in life is not the things or the money—the standard of success is absolutely the amount of joy you feel.

Appreciation and self-love are the most important aspects you could ever nurture. *Appreciation of others and the appreciation of yourself are the closest vibrational matches to Source Energy of anything we have ever witnessed anywhere in this Universe.*

If you criticize
someone or even find
fault with yourself, your result-
ing feeling would not feel good,
because this thought of criticism is so
very different from that of your Source.
In other words, because you have chosen a thought that does not match
who-you-really-are, you can, in this
moment, through your emo-
tions, feel the discord of
your choice.

We do teach
selfishness, for if you are not
selfish enough to deliberately align
with the Energy of your Source, you
have nothing to give anyway. Some worry,
"If I selfishly achieve what I want, wouldn't
I be unfairly taking it from others?" But that
concern is based on the misconception that
there is a limit of available abundance. They
worry that if they take too much of the pie,
others will be left with nothing, while,
in reality . . . *the pie expands in
proportion to the vibrational
requests of all of you.*

There are some who fear that
a selfish person may deliberately
intend harm to another, but it is not
possible for someone who is connected
to Source Energy to wish harm upon
another—for those vibrations are
not compatible.

150

If everyone on
your planet were con-
nected to their own Source
Energy, there would be no assaults,
for there would be no jealousy, insecurity, or uncomfortable feelings of competition. If everyone understood the power of
their own Being, they would not seek
to control others. Any feelings of insecurity and hatred are born from your
disconnection with who-you-are.
Your (selfish) connection with
Well-Being would bring
only Well-Being.

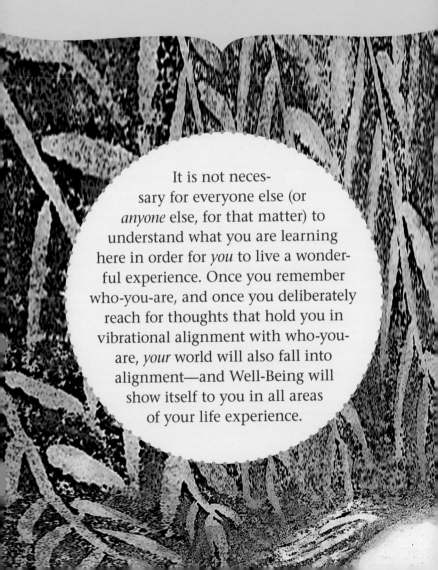

It is not neces-
sary for everyone else (or
anyone else, for that matter) to
understand what you are learning
here in order for *you* to live a wonderful experience. Once you remember
who-you-are, and once you deliberately
reach for thoughts that hold you in
vibrational alignment with who-you-
are, *your* world will also fall into
alignment—and Well-Being will
show itself to you in all areas
of your life experience.

When you want
something that you do *not*
believe is possible, when you hold
a desire for something that you do
not expect—although a strong enough
desire *can* override a weaker belief—
it does not unfold easily, for you
are not *allowing* it into your
current experience.

Unfortunately,
many people think that
the uncomfortable feeling of
wanting something they do not
expect to experience is what the feeling
of *desire* is; they no longer recognize the
feeling of pure desire as that fresh, eager
feeling of expectancy that they knew when
they were younger. The feeling of pure
desire is always delicious, as it represents
the vibrations that are stretched out
before you, into your unseen future,
preparing the way for the *Law of
Attraction* to match things
up on your behalf.

154

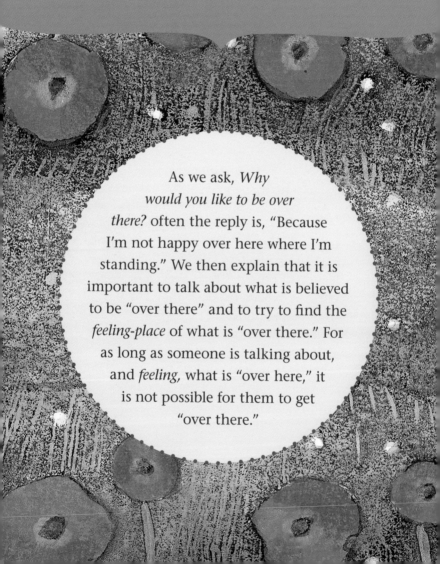

As we ask, *Why would you like to be over there?* often the reply is, "Because I'm not happy over here where I'm standing." We then explain that it is important to talk about what is believed to be "over there" and to try to find the *feeling-place* of what is "over there." For as long as someone is talking about, and *feeling*, what is "over here," it is not possible for them to get "over there."

If you have been
accustomed to thinking
and speaking about where you are
currently standing, it is not an easy
thing to suddenly shift your vibrations
and to now begin thinking and feeling
something that is very different. In fact, the
Law of Attraction says that you do not have
access to thoughts and feelings that are
very far from where you have recently
been vibrating, but, with some effort,
you could find other better-feeling
thoughts that *are* within
your reach.

With a determination to feel better, you could change the subject and therefore find other thoughts with better-feeling vibrations—but vibrational shifting is usually a gradual process. In fact, a continual attempt, in defiance of the *Law of Attraction,* to try to jump vibrational ranges is a major factor in the feelings of discouragement that eventually cause people to conclude that they really do not have control of their own life experiences.

With only a
few seconds of focusing
your attention on a subject, the
Law of Attraction begins to respond.
Within 17 seconds of focusing on
something, a matching vibration becomes
activated. And now, when you repeatedly
return to a pure thought, maintaining it
for at least 68 seconds, in a short period
of time (hours, in some cases, or a few
days in others), that thought becomes
a dominant thought. And once you
achieve a dominant thought, you
will experience matching
manifestations until you
change it.

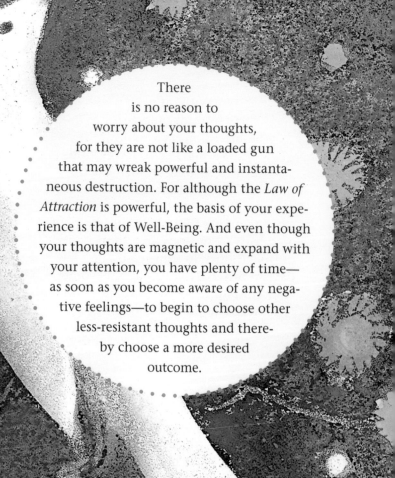

There
is no reason to
worry about your thoughts,
for they are not like a loaded gun
that may wreak powerful and instanta-
neous destruction. For although the *Law of
Attraction* is powerful, the basis of your experience is that of Well-Being. And even though
your thoughts are magnetic and expand with
your attention, you have plenty of time—
as soon as you become aware of any negative feelings—to begin to choose other
less-resistant thoughts and thereby choose a more desired
outcome.

Absolute alignment with
your own Source Energy means
that you know the following:

- You are free.
- You are powerful.
- You are good.
- You are love.
- You have value.
- You have purpose.
- All is well.

A scale of your
emotions would look
something like this:

1. Joy/Knowledge/
   Empowerment/
   Freedom/Love/
   Appreciation
2. Passion
3. Enthusiasm/
   Eagerness/
   Happiness
4. Positive
   Expectation/Belief
5. Optimism
6. Hopefulness
7. Contentment
8. Boredom
9. Pessimism
10. Frustration/Irrita-
    tion/Impatience

11. "Overwhelment"
12. Disappointment
13. Doubt
14. Worry
15. Blame
16. Discouragement
17. Anger
18. Revenge
19. Hatred/Rage
20. Jealousy
21. Insecurity/Guilt/
    Unworthiness
22. Fear/Grief/
    Depression/Despair/
    Powerlessness

Word labels for
your emotions are not
absolutely accurate for every
person who feels the emotion. In fact,
giving word labels to the emotions could
cause confusion and distract you from the
real purpose of your *Emotional Guidance
Scale*. The thing that matters most is that
you consciously reach for a feeling that
is improved. The word for the
feeling is not important.

There are so many
who have convinced you that
your *anger* is inappropriate—but, of
course, they cannot feel the improvement that the *angry* thought really is. But
when you *consciously* know that you have
chosen an *angry* thought that has brought you
relief, then you can consciously know that you
can move from the *angry* thought to a less-
resistant one, such as *frustration,* and then
up the *Emotional Guidance Scale* you
go—right back into your full
alignment.

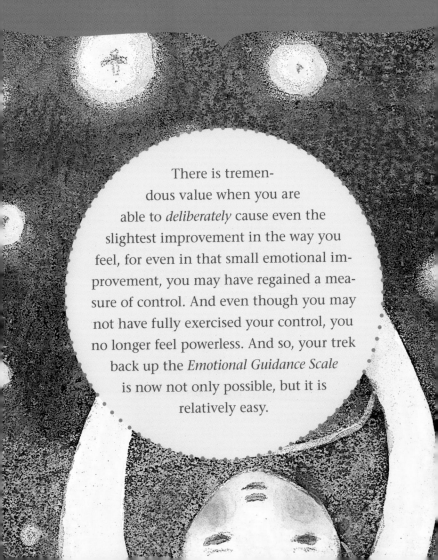

There is tremen-
dous value when you are
able to *deliberately* cause even the
slightest improvement in the way you
feel, for even in that small emotional improvement, you may have regained a mea-
sure of control. And even though you may
not have fully exercised your control, you
no longer feel powerless. And so, your trek
back up the *Emotional Guidance Scale*
is now not only possible, but it is
relatively easy.

Someone outside of you
does not know if your chosen
thought of anger is an improvement
for you; only you know—by the relief
that you feel—the appropriateness of any
thought. Until you decide that you are
going to guide yourself by the way you
feel, you can make no steady prog-
ress toward your own desires.

A key to regain-
ing your wonderful feeling
of personal empowerment and
control is to decide, right now, no
matter how good or how bad you are
feeling, that you are going to do your best
to make the best of it. Reach for the best-
feeling thought that you have access to
right now; and as you do that again and
again, in a short period of time you
will find yourself in a very good-
feeling place. That is just the
way it works!

Desire, for many people, often feels like yearning, for while they are focused upon something that they want to experience or have, they are equally aware of its absence. And so, while they are using *words of desire,* they are offering a *vibration of lack.* They come to think that the *feeling of desire* is like wanting something that they do not have. But there is no feeling of lack in pure desire. . . . *If you will keep in mind that whenever you ask, it is always given, then each of your desires will now be pure, unresisted desire.*

There have been
some who have said to us,
"Abraham, I've been taught that
it's not appropriate for me to have
any desires. I've been taught that the
state of desire will keep me from being the
'Spiritual Being' that I'm supposed to be,
and that my state of happiness depends
upon my ability to release all desires."
We reply, *But is not your state of
happiness, or your state of
spirituality, a <u>desire?</u>*

168

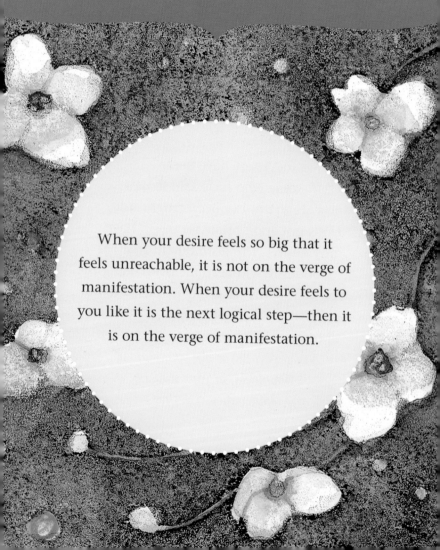

When your desire feels so big that it feels unreachable, it is not on the verge of manifestation. When your desire feels to you like it is the next logical step—then it is on the verge of manifestation.

You can tell by
the way you *feel* whether
your vibration is in the place
where you are allowing Universal
Forces to deliver your desire to you
now—or not. With practice, you will know
whether you are on the brink of a manifestation or whether it is still in the becoming stages; but, most important, *once
you are in control of the way you feel,
you will enjoy it all. . . .*

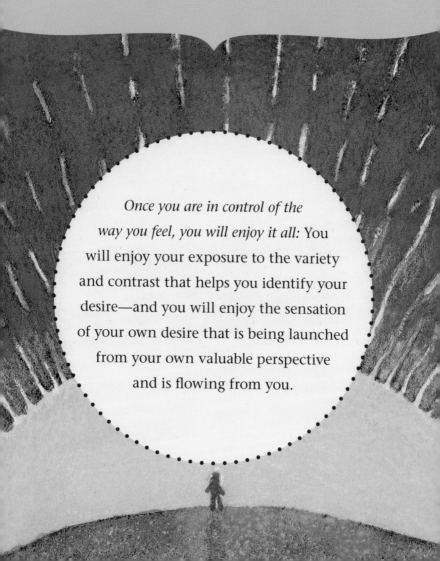

170

Once you are in control of the way you feel, you will enjoy it all: You will enjoy your exposure to the variety and contrast that helps you identify your desire—and you will enjoy the sensation of your own desire that is being launched from your own valuable perspective and is flowing from you.

*Once you are in control
of the way you feel, you will
enjoy it all:* You will enjoy the sensation of your conscious awareness when
you are not a vibrational match to your
own desire—and you will enjoy the sensation of deliberately bringing yourself
back into vibrational alignment
with your desire.

*Once you are in control of the
way you feel, you will enjoy it all:* You
will feel relief as doubts slip away and
as the secure feelings of Well-Being
replace them.

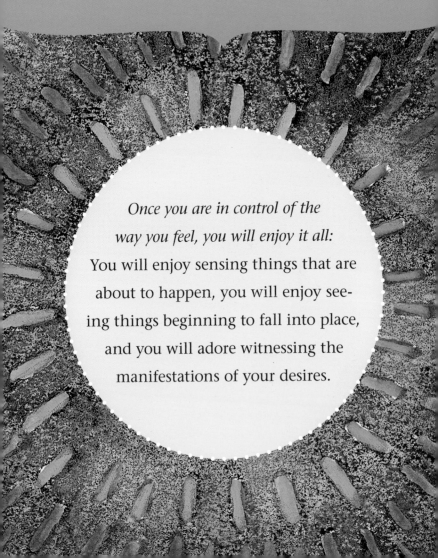

173

*Once you are in control of the
way you feel, you will enjoy it all:*
You will enjoy sensing things that are
about to happen, you will enjoy seeing things beginning to fall into place,
and you will adore witnessing the
manifestations of your desires.

*Once you are in control of the
way you feel, you will enjoy it all:*
You will revel in the conscious awareness that you have deliberately molded
your desires into being in as real a way
as if you had created a statue with
the clay in your own hands.

Once you are in control of the way you feel, you will enjoy it all: You will adore the sensations you feel as you align, again and again, with the fruits of your own experience.

The entire Universe exists to produce new life-giving desire within you; and when you go with the flow of your own desires, you will feel truly alive—and you will truly live.

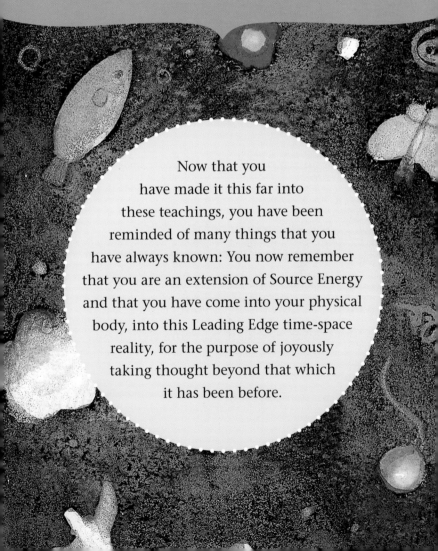

Now that you
have made it this far into
these teachings, you have been
reminded of many things that you
have always known: You now remember
that you are an extension of Source Energy
and that you have come into your physical
body, into this Leading Edge time-space
reality, for the purpose of joyously
taking thought beyond that which
it has been before.

You now remember that you have
an *Emotional Guidance System* within
you that helps you to know, in every
moment, how much of your connection to
your Source you are allowing right now.

You now remember that the
better you feel, the more you are
in alignment with who-you-really-are;
and the worse you feel, the more you
are disallowing that important
connection.

You now remember that there is nothing that you cannot be, do, or have; and you remember that if your dominant intention is to feel good—and that if you try to make the best of where you are—you must reach your natural state of joy.

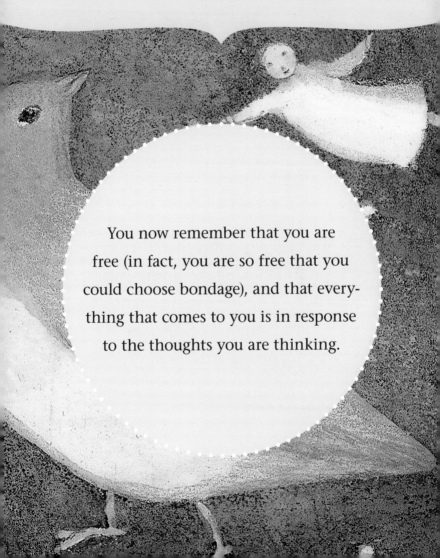

You now remember that you are free (in fact, you are so free that you could choose bondage), and that everything that comes to you is in response to the thoughts you are thinking.

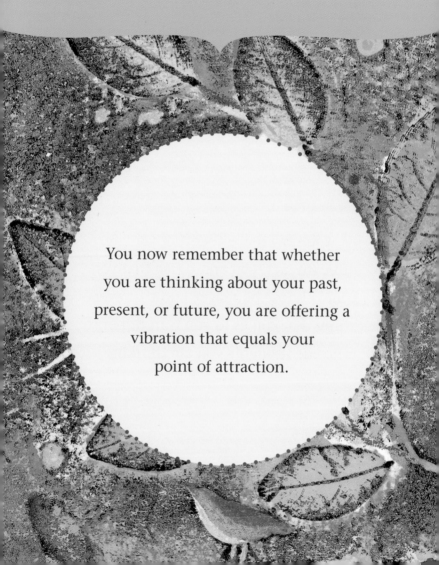

182

You now remember that whether
you are thinking about your past,
present, or future, you are offering a
vibration that equals your
point of attraction.

183

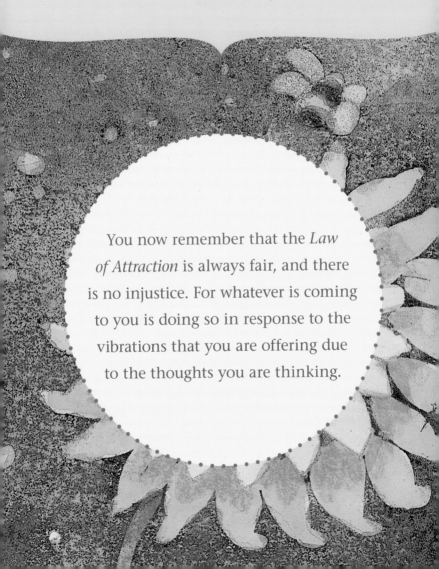

You now remember that the *Law of Attraction* is always fair, and there is no injustice. For whatever is coming to you is doing so in response to the vibrations that you are offering due to the thoughts you are thinking.

And, most
important, you now remem-
ber that Well-Being is the basis of
your world, and that unless you are
doing something that is disallowing it,
then Well-Being is your experience. You
may allow it or resist it, but only a Stream
of wellness, abundance, clarity,
and all good things that you
desire . . . flows.

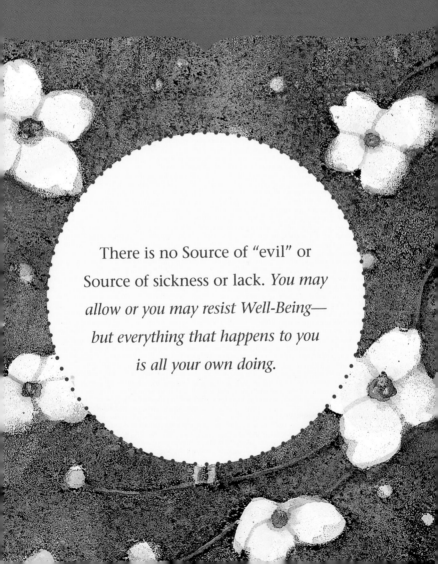

There is no Source of "evil" or
Source of sickness or lack. *You may
allow or you may resist Well-Being—
but everything that happens to you
is all your own doing.*

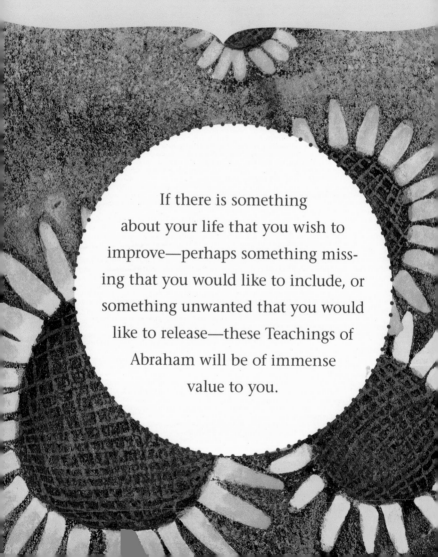

186

If there is something
about your life that you wish to
improve—perhaps something missing that you would like to include, or
something unwanted that you would
like to release—these Teachings of
Abraham will be of immense
value to you.

Your habit of resistant
thought is the only thing that
ever keeps you from allowing the
things you desire. And although you
certainly did not intentionally develop
these resistant patterns of thought, you
did pick them up along your physical trail,
bit by bit, and experience by experience.
But one thing is very clear: *If you do not
do something that causes a different
vibrational offering, then nothing in
your experience can change.*

188

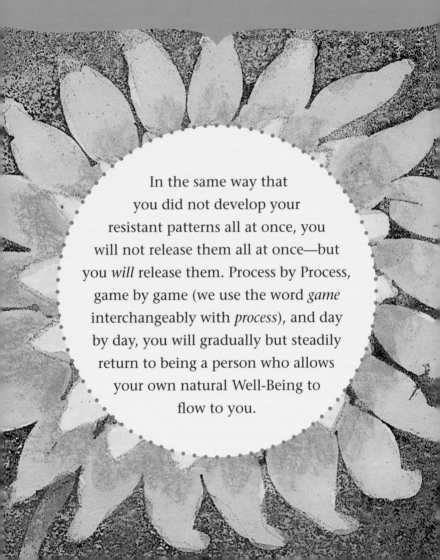

In the same way that
you did not develop your
resistant patterns all at once, you
will not release them all at once—but
you *will* release them. Process by Process,
game by game (we use the word *game*
interchangeably with *process*), and day
by day, you will gradually but steadily
return to being a person who allows
your own natural Well-Being to
flow to you.

Those who observe you
will be amazed by the things
they begin to see happening in your
experience and by the joy that you will
obviously be radiating. And you will explain, with the confidence and certainty
that you were born with, "I have found a
way to allow the Well-Being flow that
is natural to me. I have learned to
practice the *Art of Allowing*."

The processes presented in these
Teachings of Abraham are designed to
help you remove the resistance from your
path, for there is nothing more delicious
than moving at the speed of life that you
are accustomed to—with no trees
in the way.

The most important
thing for you to acknowledge
before you apply any of these
processes is how you are feeling right
now—and how you would like to feel. At
the beginning of each process, we indicate
an emotional range that we suggest for
each one. Any of the processes that fall
within the emotional range that you
believe you are feeling right now
is a perfect place to begin.

It is our absolute promise to you that your life will improve with the application of these teachings, for you cannot apply them without improving the way you feel. And you cannot improve the way you feel without releasing resistance and thereby improving your point of attraction. And when you improve your point of attraction, the *Law of Attraction* must bring you circumstances, events, relationships, experiences, sensations, and powerful evidence of your shift in vibration.
It is *Law!*

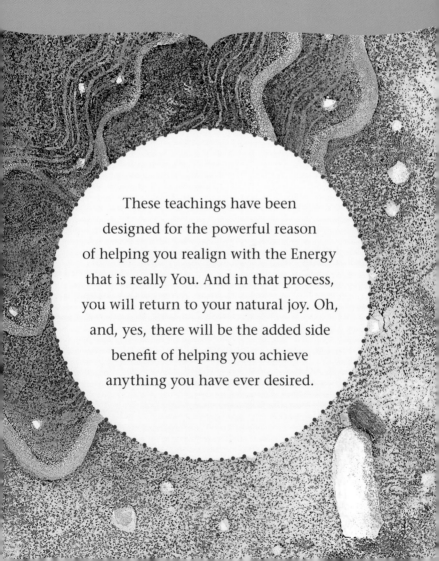

These teachings have been
designed for the powerful reason
of helping you realign with the Energy
that is really You. And in that process,
you will return to your natural joy. Oh,
and, yes, there will be the added side
benefit of helping you achieve
anything you have ever desired.

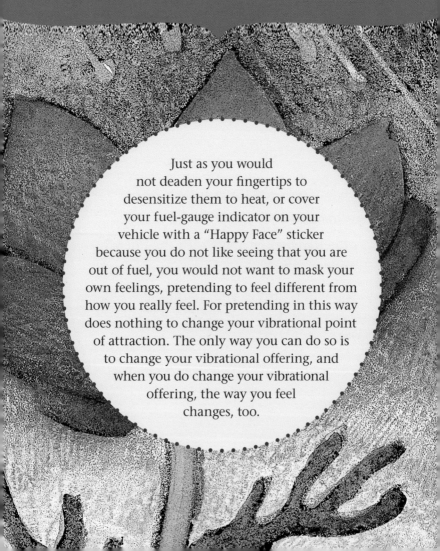

Just as you would
not deaden your fingertips to
desensitize them to heat, or cover
your fuel-gauge indicator on your
vehicle with a "Happy Face" sticker
because you do not like seeing that you are
out of fuel, you would not want to mask your
own feelings, pretending to feel different from
how you really feel. For pretending in this way
does nothing to change your vibrational point
of attraction. The only way you can do so is
to change your vibrational offering, and
when you do change your vibrational
offering, the way you feel
changes, too.

When
you remember an
incident from a past experience, you are focusing Energy.
When you are imagining something
that may occur in your future, you are
also focusing Energy. And, of course, when
you are observing something in your *now,*
you are focusing Energy. It makes no difference whether you are focusing on the past,
present, or future . . . you are still focusing
Energy—and your point of attention,
or focus, is causing you to offer a
vibration that is your point of
attraction.

There are two
surefire ways to understand
what your vibrational offering
is: Notice what is happening in your
experience (for what you are focused
upon and what is manifesting are always
a vibrational match), and notice how you
feel (because your emotions are giving
you constant feedback about your
vibrational offering and your
point of attraction).

The most satisfying aspect of *Deliberate Creation* comes from being sensitive to the way the thoughts you are thinking feel, for then it is possible to modify a bad-feeling thought to one that feels better, and to thereby improve your point of attraction before something unwanted manifests. *It is far easier—before an unwanted physical manifestation appears—to deliberately change the direction of your thought to something that feels better.*

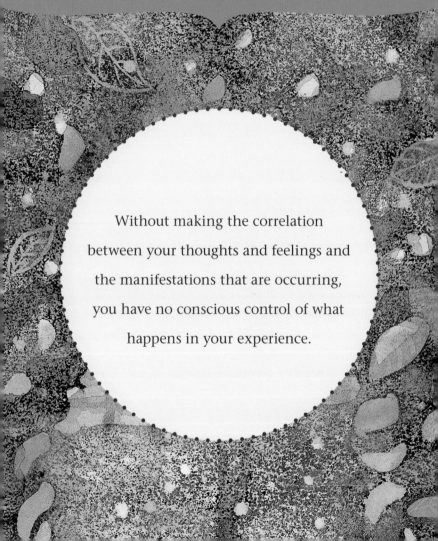

Without making the correlation
between your thoughts and feelings and
the manifestations that are occurring,
you have no conscious control of what
happens in your experience.

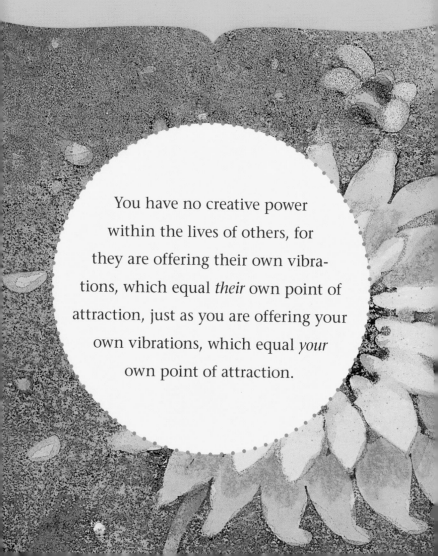

You have no creative power within the lives of others, for they are offering their own vibrations, which equal *their* own point of attraction, just as you are offering your own vibrations, which equal *your* own point of attraction.

Deliberate Creation is not
about the condition changing
and then your finding a better feeling in response to the changed condition. *Deliberate Creation* is about choosing a thought that feels good when
you choose it—which then causes
the condition to change.

Unconditional
love is really about wanting
so much to remain in connection
with your Source of love that you deliberately choose thoughts that allow your
connection (no matter what manifestations
may be happening nearby). And when you
are able to control your point of attraction
by deliberately choosing better-feeling
thoughts, the conditions that surround
you have to change. The *Law
of Attraction* says that
they must.

Remember that the *Law of Attraction* is a powerful *Law,* and that it is not possible for you to find and hold a thought if your current *vibrational set-point* is very different from that thought. *You only have access to thoughts whose vibrations are somewhere in your current vibrational range.*

There are times
when friends can prod or
tease you into a better-feeling
thought, but at other times their
prodding or teasing just makes you feel
worse. Any success they may have had in
helping you feel better has been, for the most
part, about how far out of alignment you
already were, because while it is easy to
make small vibrational jumps, it is
difficult, or even impossible,
to make large ones.

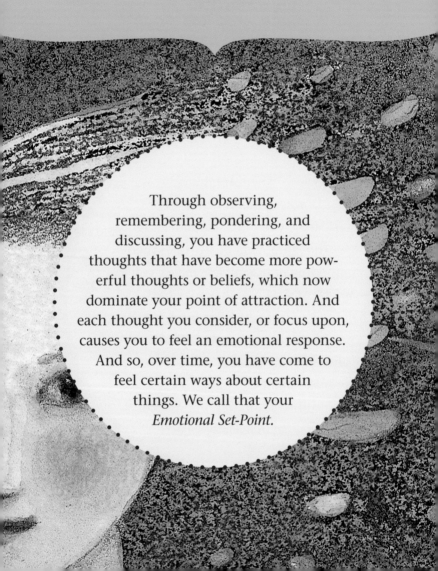

204

Through observing, remembering, pondering, and discussing, you have practiced thoughts that have become more powerful thoughts or beliefs, which now dominate your point of attraction. And each thought you consider, or focus upon, causes you to feel an emotional response. And so, over time, you have come to feel certain ways about certain things. We call that your *Emotional Set-Point.*

It does not matter
how good you feel or how
fast you feel it—the only thing
that matters is that you *consciously*
discover some relief, no matter how slight
it is, and that you understand that your
relief has come in response to some *deliberate*
effort that you have offered. For when you
are able to consciously find relief, then you
have regained creative control of your
own experience, and then you are
on your way to wherever you
wish to go.

You are the creator of
your own experience whether
you know that you are or not. Your
life experience is unfolding in precise
response to the vibrations that radiate
as a result of your thoughts—whether
you know that it is or not.

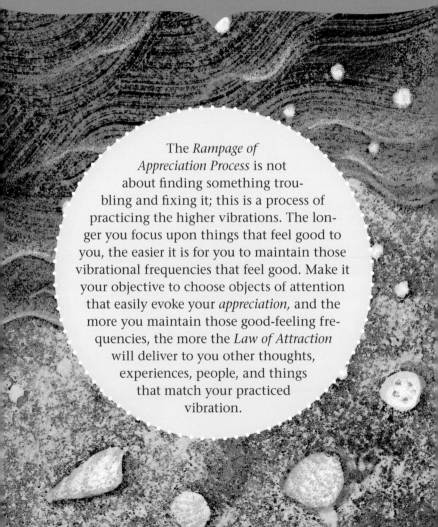

The *Rampage of Appreciation Process* is not about finding something troubling and fixing it; this is a process of practicing the higher vibrations. The longer you focus upon things that feel good to you, the easier it is for you to maintain those vibrational frequencies that feel good. Make it your objective to choose objects of attention that easily evoke your *appreciation,* and the more you maintain those good-feeling frequencies, the more the *Law of Attraction* will deliver to you other thoughts, experiences, people, and things that match your practiced vibration.

Once it is your
primary intention, as you
move through your day, to find
things to *appreciate,* you are practicing a vibration of less resistance, and
you are making your connection to your
own Source Energy stronger. Because the
vibration of *appreciation* is the most powerful connection between the physical you
and the Non-Physical You, this process
will also put you in a position to
receive even clearer guidance
from your Inner Being.

The more you practice *appreciation*, the less resistance you will have in your own vibrational frequencies; and the less resistance you have, the better your life will be. Also, by practicing a *Rampage of Appreciation*, you will become accustomed to the feeling of higher vibrations, so that if you ever revert to an old pattern of conversation that causes resistance in your vibration, you will notice it early on, before the vibration gets too strong.

The more you
find something to *appreci-
ate,* the better it feels; the better
it feels, the more you want to do it;
the more you do it, the better it feels;
the better it feels . . . the more you want
to do it. The *Law of Attraction* assists with
the powerful momentum of these positive thoughts and feelings until—with
very little time and effort—you will
find your heart singing in your
joyous alignment with
who-you-really-are.

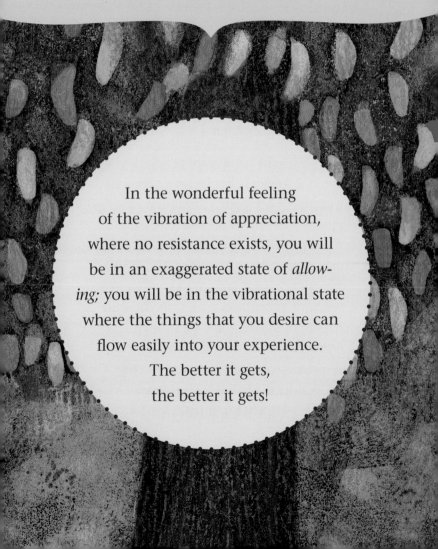

211

In the wonderful feeling
of the vibration of appreciation,
where no resistance exists, you will
be in an exaggerated state of *allowing;* you will be in the vibrational state
where the things that you desire can
flow easily into your experience.
The better it gets,
the better it gets!

In the *Rampage of Appreciation Process,* you actually set your vibrational frequency to one of allowing what you have asked for into your experience. You have been asking, in every day of your experience, and Source has answered, without exception. And now, in your mode of *appreciation,* you are in the practice of receiving. You are now engaging in the last step in the process of *Creation* (you are letting it in).

213

Once you
become oriented toward
looking for things to *appreciate*,
you will find that your day will be
filled with such things. Your thoughts
and feelings of *appreciation* will flow from
you naturally. And, often, while in the
midst of a genuine feeling of *appreciation*
for someone or something, you will feel
ripples of thrill bumps—those sensations are confirming your alignment with your Source.

Every time you *appreciate*
something, every time you *praise*
something, every time you *feel good*
about something, you are telling the
Universe: "More of this, please." You need
never make another verbal statement of
an intent—*and if you are mostly in a
state of appreciation, all good things
will flow to you.*

We are often asked, *Isn't <u>love</u> a better word than <u>appreciation?</u> Isn't <u>love</u> more descriptive of the Non-Physical Energy?* And we say that *love* and *appreciation* are really the same vibration. Some use the word *gratitude,* or a feeling of *thankfulness,* for all of these words are descriptive of Well-Being.

A desire to *appreciate* is a very good first step; and then as you find more things that you would like to feel appreciation for, it quickly gains momentum. And as you want to feel appreciation, you *attract* something to *appreciate*. And as you *appreciate* it, then you attract something else to *appreciate,* until, in time, you are experiencing a *Rampage of Appreciation*.

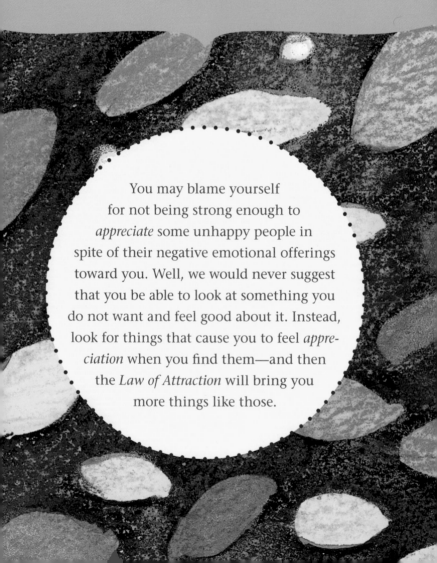

You may blame yourself
for not being strong enough to
appreciate some unhappy people in
spite of their negative emotional offerings
toward you. Well, we would never suggest
that you be able to look at something you
do not want and feel good about it. Instead,
look for things that cause you to feel *appreciation* when you find them—and then
the *Law of Attraction* will bring you
more things like those.

218

Whenever you are
looking for things to
appreciate, you have control of
your own vibrational offering and your
own point of attraction; but when you are
responding to the way others seem to feel
about you, you have no control. . . . You do
not know what happened to them today, and
you do not how they are living, so you cannot understand why they react to you in the
way they do—and you cannot control it.
However, when you are more interested
in how *you* feel than how they feel
about you, you do have control
of your experience.

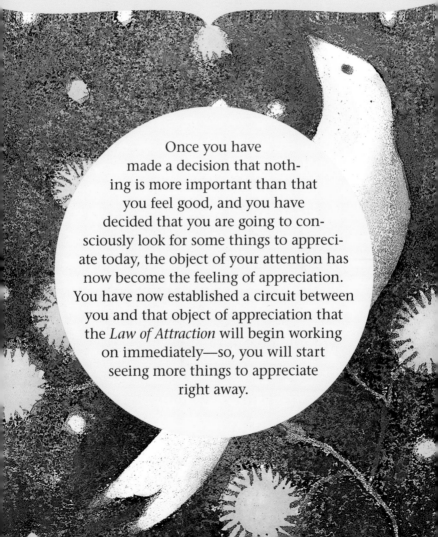

Once you have made a decision that nothing is more important than that you feel good, and you have decided that you are going to consciously look for some things to appreciate today, the object of your attention has now become the feeling of appreciation. You have now established a circuit between you and that object of appreciation that the *Law of Attraction* will begin working on immediately—so, you will start seeing more things to appreciate right away.

We want you to feel the value of connecting with Non-Physical Energy—and *appreciation* is the easiest and fastest way. When your desire to connect with the Non-Physical Energy is sufficient, you will find dozens of ways, in every hour, to make your *appreciation* flow.

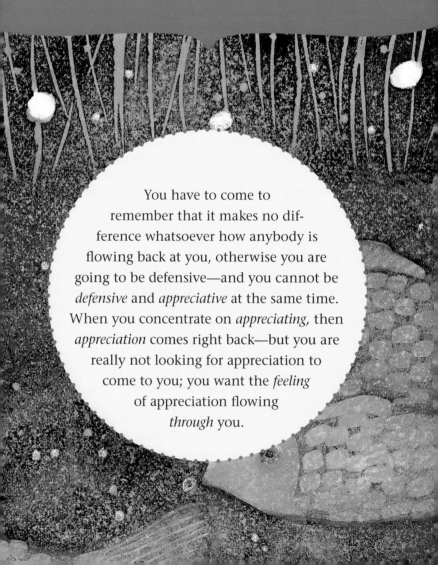

You have to come to
remember that it makes no difference whatsoever how anybody is
flowing back at you, otherwise you are
going to be defensive—and you cannot be
defensive and *appreciative* at the same time.
When you concentrate on *appreciating,* then
appreciation comes right back—but you are
really not looking for appreciation to
come to you; you want the *feeling*
of appreciation flowing
through you.

222

As you move
through your day and as
you become aware of something
that you do *not* want, your desire about
what you *do* want comes into clearer focus.
And now, when you have been practicing a
Rampage of Appreciation, you can easily re-
focus your awareness of what you do not
want into your awareness of what you
do want. Now you are the hands-on
creator that you have come
forth to be.

Life is not about tomorrow;
it is about right now. Life is
about how you are currently
molding the Energy!

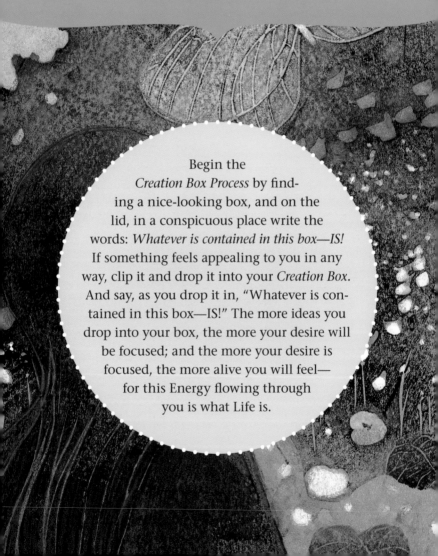

224

Begin the
Creation Box Process by finding a nice-looking box, and on the
lid, in a conspicuous place write the
words: *Whatever is contained in this box—IS!*
If something feels appealing to you in any
way, clip it and drop it into your *Creation Box*.
And say, as you drop it in, "Whatever is contained in this box—IS!" The more ideas you
drop into your box, the more your desire will
be focused; and the more your desire is
focused, the more alive you will feel—
for this Energy flowing through
you is what Life is.

225

For someone who has not been practicing thoughts of resistance, the *Creation Box Process* will be all that you will ever need to create a wonderful life: You ask; Source answers; you let it in. *You ask and it is given.*

Most people offer most
of their vibrational offerings in
response to what they are observing,
but there is no creative control in that.
Your creative control comes only in
deliberately offering thought—and
when you are visualizing, you
have complete control.

Once you begin the *Creation Box Process*, you will just be knocked over by the effectiveness and efficiency of the enormous Non-Physical staff who responds to your vibrational requests. When you ask, it is given; and as you play with the *Creation Box Process*, you will learn to let it in.

When you identi-
fy any of the four basic subjects of your life—Body, Home,
Relationships, or Work—a focusing of
Energy occurs. When you make more specific statements of desire, you activate the
Energy around those subjects even more. And
when you think about *why* you want those
things, you can usually be softening your resistance around the subject while adding even
more clarity and power to the thoughts.
Why you want something defines the
essence of the *what* you want. . . .
*The Universe always delivers to you
the vibrational essence of
your desire.*

Why you want something
defines the essence of the *what* you
want, and the Universe always delivers to you the vibrational essence of your
desire. . . . So, when you think about *why* you
want something, you usually soften resistance;
but when you think about *when* it will come
to you or *how* it will come or *who* will help it
to come, you often add resistance, espe-
cially if you do not already know the
answers to those questions.

230

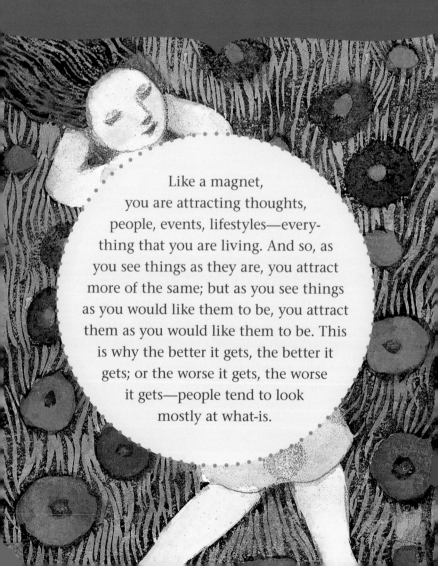

Like a magnet,
you are attracting thoughts,
people, events, lifestyles—everything that you are living. And so, as
you see things as they are, you attract
more of the same; but as you see things
as you would like them to be, you attract
them as you would like them to be. This
is why the better it gets, the better it
gets; or the worse it gets, the worse
it gets—people tend to look
mostly at what-is.

We are offering
processes whereby you may
spend a little bit of time, every
day, *intentionally* attracting into your
experience good health, vitality, prosperity, and positive interactions with
others—all the things that make up
your vision of what the perfect life
experience for you would be.

Remember,
you live in a Vibrational
Universe, and all things are
managed by the *Law of Attraction*.
And you get what you think about,
whether you want it or not, because
whenever you achieve vibrational harmony with something because you are
giving it your attention, the vibrational essence of it will, in some
way, begin to show up in
your life experience.

The Universe
responds to your vibra-
tional offering, to your point of
attraction, to the thoughts you think,
and to the way you feel. The Universe
is not responding to what *has* been manifested in your experience, but, instead, to
the vibration that you are *now* offering. The
Universe makes no distinction between
your actually having a million dollars and
your giving thought to having a
million dollars—*your point of attraction is about your thoughts, not
about your manifestations.*

The *Virtual Reality Process* is not one where you try to fix something that is broken. It is one where you deliberately activate a scene in your own mind that causes you to offer a vibration matching the scene you have activated in your visualization—and as you practice visualizing pleasant scenes in your mind, these good-feeling vibrations can then become your new *set-point*.

Remember, the *Creative Process* comprises three steps: (1) Ask (that's easy—you do it all the time). (2) Answer the asking (that is not your work—Source Energy does that). (3) Allow (be in the receiving mode of what you are asking for).

It is important
that you realize that Steps
1 and 3 of the *Creative Process*
are different. When you are focused
upon, or praying for, something you
really want or need, often you are not
a vibrational match *to the thing you
want.* Instead, you are a match to
the absence of *the thing
you want.*

You are continu-
ally *asking.* You cannot stop
asking; contrast is evoking the
desire from you. Your real work is to
find a way to be in the receiving mode. It
is similar to wanting to receive a satellite or
radio signal. To do so, you have to set your
receiver on the same wavelength as the trans-
mitter or you are going to get static; you are
not going to get a clear signal. In like manner, you recognize the alignment of your
(transmitted and received) signals by
feeling the alignment of
your emotions.

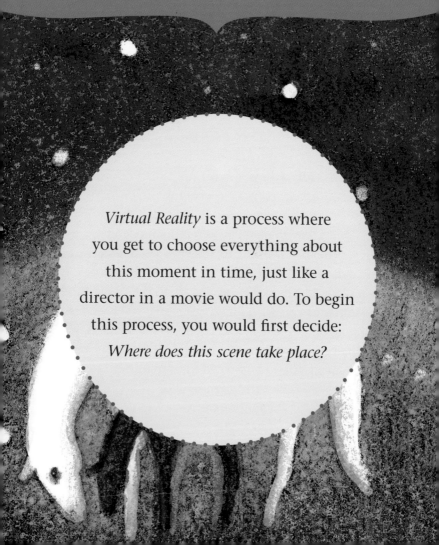

238

Virtual Reality is a process where you get to choose everything about this moment in time, just like a director in a movie would do. To begin this process, you would first decide: *Where does this scene take place?*

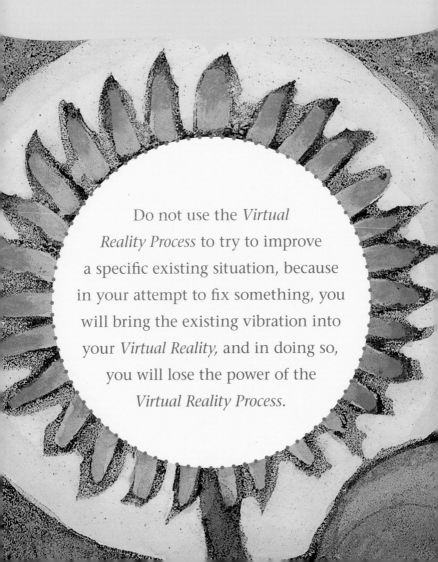

Do not use the *Virtual
Reality Process* to try to improve
a specific existing situation, because
in your attempt to fix something, you
will bring the existing vibration into
your *Virtual Reality,* and in doing so,
you will lose the power of the
Virtual Reality Process.

There is no reason why Well-Being is not pouring into your experience—in precise detail in response to all of the things that you have identified that you want—other than the fact that you are in a bad mood, or are angry or worried about something.

As you create scenarios
that make you feel good, you
activate a vibration that *does* feel
good, and then the *Law of Attraction*
matches that vibration. *There is nothing
more important than that you feel good—
and there is nothing better than creating images that cause you to
feel good.*

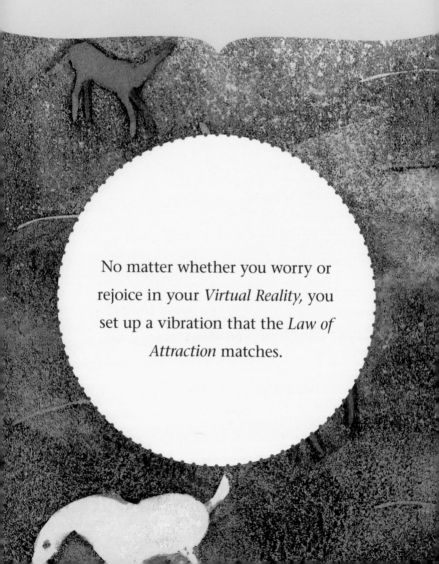

No matter whether you worry or rejoice in your *Virtual Reality,* you set up a vibration that the *Law of Attraction* matches.

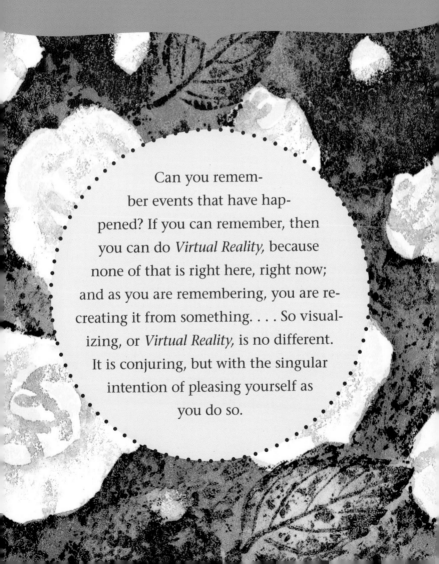

Can you remem-
ber events that have hap-
pened? If you can remember, then
you can do *Virtual Reality,* because
none of that is right here, right now;
and as you are remembering, you are re-
creating it from something. . . . So visualizing, or *Virtual Reality,* is no different.
It is conjuring, but with the singular
intention of pleasing yourself as
you do so.

244

As you practice
visualizing, and stimu-
late your imagination more,
you will not only find the process
to be a delightful, good-feeling way
to spend some time, you will discover
that your dominant vibration, on a
myriad of subjects, is changing—and
your life experience will now begin
to reflect these wonderful
improvements.

Any thought
that you continue to think
is called a *belief*. And many of
your beliefs serve you extremely
well: thoughts that harmonize with the
knowledge of your Source, and thoughts
that match the desires that you hold. . . .
But some of your beliefs do *not* serve you
well: Thoughts about your own inad-
equacy or your unworthiness are
examples of those kinds
of thoughts.

With an
understanding of the *Laws
of the Universe* and some willing-
ness to deliberately choose thoughts,
you can, in time, replace all hindering
beliefs with life-giving beliefs; but there is
a process that can give you the immediate benefit of changing your beliefs, in
a much shorter time—we call this
the *Process of Meditation*.

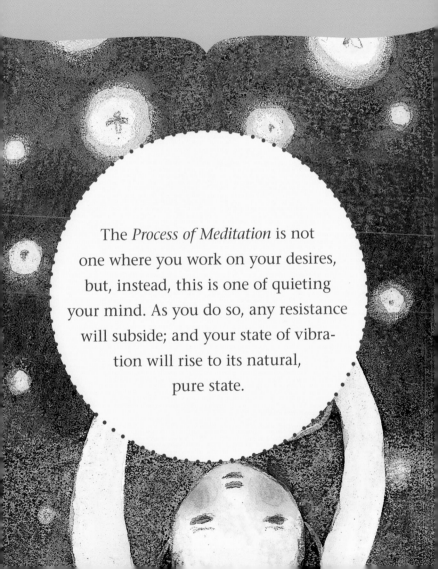

The *Process of Meditation* is not
one where you work on your desires,
but, instead, this is one of quieting
your mind. As you do so, any resistance
will subside; and your state of vibration will rise to its natural,
pure state.

There are other
ways of raising your vibrations than meditation, such as
listening to music that makes your
heart sing, jogging in a beautiful place,
petting your cat, walking your dog, and so
on. Often you are in your highest state of connection to Source Energy while you are driving
your vehicle. Your goal is to release any thought
that causes resistance so that you are then in a
place of pure, positive thought. Just find any
thought that feels good when you think
it, and practice it until you begin to set
that tone within you—and then,
other good-feeling thoughts
will follow.

If we were in your physical shoes, we would sit quietly, by ourselves, in some pleasant place where we would not be interrupted—maybe under a tree, maybe in our vehicle, maybe in the bathroom or garden—and we would utilize 10 or 15 minutes, and not much more time than that, to quiet our mind in meditation.

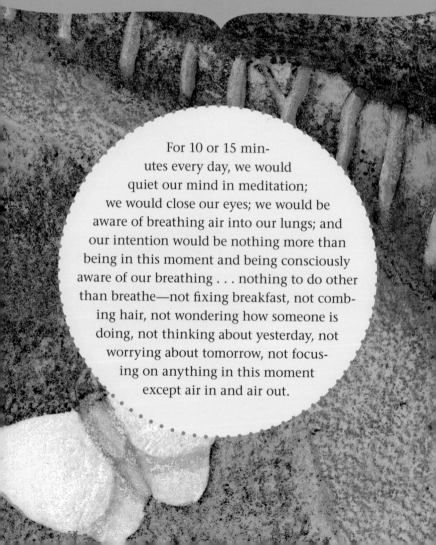

For 10 or 15 min-
utes every day, we would
quiet our mind in meditation;
we would close our eyes; we would be
aware of breathing air into our lungs; and
our intention would be nothing more than
being in this moment and being consciously
aware of our breathing . . . nothing to do other
than breathe—not fixing breakfast, not comb-
ing hair, not wondering how someone is
doing, not thinking about yesterday, not
worrying about tomorrow, not focusing on anything in this moment
except air in and air out.

Meditation is a
state of *allowing* where, for
just a few moments, you stop trying to make anything happen. It is a
time when you are saying to your *Source
Energy,* to your *Inner Being,* to your *God* (or
whatever you want to call it): *Here I am, in
a state of allowing Source Energy to flow purely
through me.* Fifteen minutes of effort will
change your life. It will allow the Energy
that is natural to you to flow; you will
feel better in the moment, and you
will feel more energized when
you come out of it.

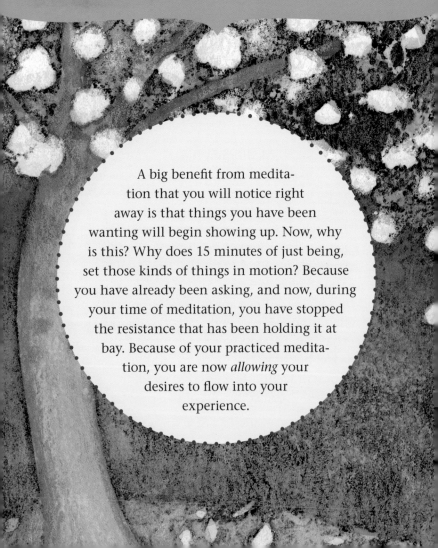

A big benefit from meditation that you will notice right away is that things you have been wanting will begin showing up. Now, why is this? Why does 15 minutes of just being, set those kinds of things in motion? Because you have already been asking, and now, during your time of meditation, you have stopped the resistance that has been holding it at bay. Because of your practiced meditation, you are now *allowing* your desires to flow into your experience.

You cannot be part
of this physical environ-
ment without endless desires
being born within you. And as these
desires are being born within you, the
Universe is answering them. And now,
because of 15 minutes of *allowing,* whether
you were petting the cat, practicing your
breathing in meditation, listening to a
waterfall or soothing music, or were on
a *Rampage of Appreciation* . . . during
that time of *allowing* you established
a vibration that no longer caused
resistance to the things
that you have been
asking for.

"Well, what if I've really developed major habits of negativity? Is 15 minutes going to change that?" *Probably not right away. But the next time you go to one of those negative thoughts, you are going to be more aware of it. Your <u>Guidance System</u> is going to be stimulated so that you will be aware—probably for the first time in your life—of what you are doing with your Non-Physical Energy.*

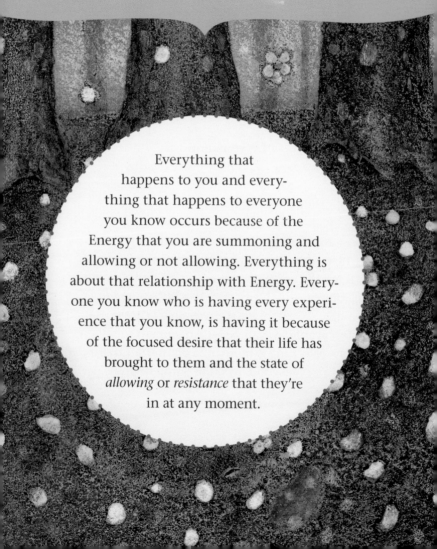

Everything that
happens to you and every-
thing that happens to everyone
you know occurs because of the
Energy that you are summoning and
allowing or not allowing. Everything is
about that relationship with Energy. Everyone you know who is having every experience that you know, is having it because
of the focused desire that their life has
brought to them and the state of
allowing or *resistance* that they're
in at any moment.

Do you know that
you could have every deadly
disease known to man (and some
they have not even figured out yet) in
your body right now, and tomorrow they
could all be gone if—from one day to the
next—you learned how to allow the Energy to
flow? We are really not encouraging those kinds
of quantum leaps; they're a little uncomfortable. What we *are* really encouraging is that,
every day, you be selfish enough to say,
"Nothing is more important than that
I feel good. And I'm going to find
ways to do so today."

"I'm going to begin my day by meditating and bringing myself into alignment with my Source Energy. And as I move through the day, I'm going to look for opportunities to *appreciate,* so that all day long I'll bring myself back into Source Energy. If there's an opportunity to praise, I'm going to praise; if there's an opportunity to criticize, I'm going to keep my mouth shut and try to meditate. If I feel like criticizing, I'll say, 'Here kitty, kitty,' and I'll pet my cat till that feeling goes away."

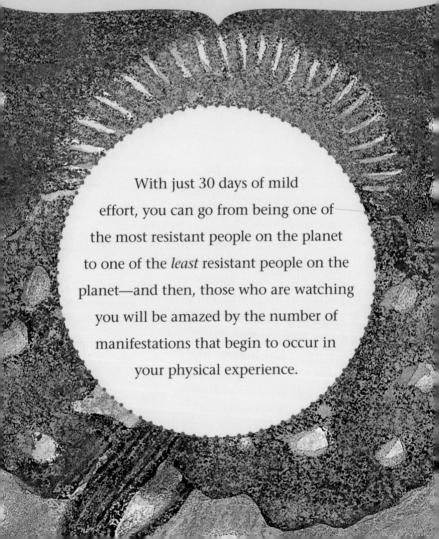

With just 30 days of mild
effort, you can go from being one of
the most resistant people on the planet
to one of the *least* resistant people on the
planet—and then, those who are watching
you will be amazed by the number of
manifestations that begin to occur in
your physical experience.

We sort of see
you from an aerial view,
and it is like you are standing on
one side of a closed door, and on the
other side are all the things you have
been wanting, just leaning up against the
door, waiting for you to open it. They have
been there from the first moment you
asked for them: your lovers, your perfect
bodies, your ideal jobs, all the money
that you could ever imagine—
all the things that you
have ever wanted!

260

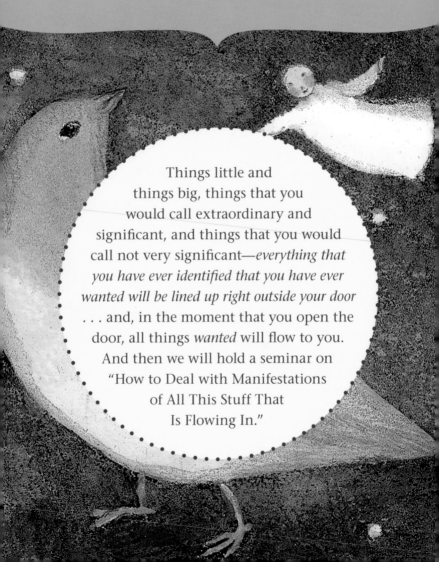

Things little and
things big, things that you
would call extraordinary and
significant, and things that you would
call not very significant—*everything that
you have ever identified that you have ever
wanted will be lined up right outside your door
. . . and, in the moment that you open the
door, all things *wanted* will flow to you.
And then we will hold a seminar on
"How to Deal with Manifestations
of All This Stuff That
Is Flowing In."

What you think about and what manifests in your life experience is always a vibrational match; and in the same way, what you think about and what manifests in your dream state is always a vibrational match.

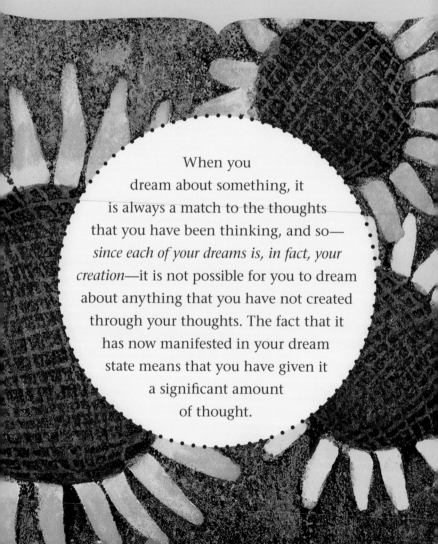

When you
dream about something, it
is always a match to the thoughts
that you have been thinking, and so—
*since each of your dreams is, in fact, your
creation*—it is not possible for you to dream
about anything that you have not created
through your thoughts. The fact that it
has now manifested in your dream
state means that you have given it
a significant amount
of thought.

The essence of the way
you feel about the things you
think about most will eventually
manifest in your real-life experience—
but it takes even *less* time and attention
for it to manifest in your dream state.
And for that reason, *your dreams can be
of immense value in helping you understand what you are in the process of
creating in your awake state.*

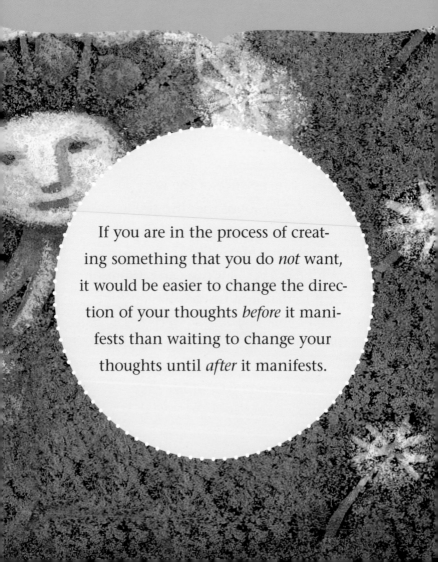

If you are in the process of creating something that you do *not* want, it would be easier to change the direction of your thoughts *before* it manifests than waiting to change your thoughts until *after* it manifests.

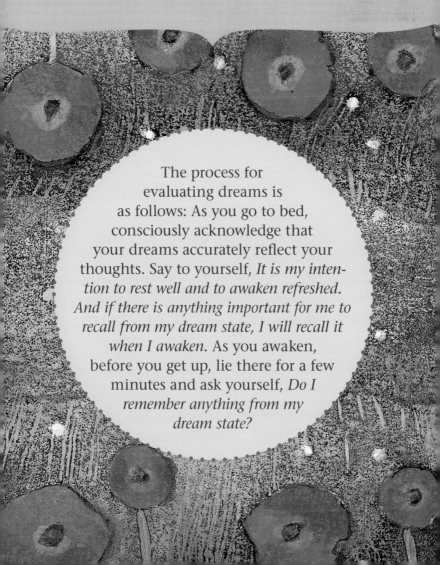

265

The process for
evaluating dreams is
as follows: As you go to bed,
consciously acknowledge that
your dreams accurately reflect your
thoughts. Say to yourself, *It is my intention to rest well and to awaken refreshed.
And if there is anything important for me to
recall from my dream state, I will recall it
when I awaken.* As you awaken,
before you get up, lie there for a few
minutes and ask yourself, *Do I
remember anything from my
dream state?*

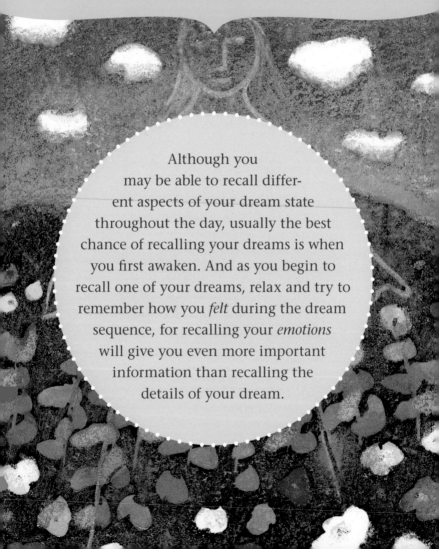

266

Although you
may be able to recall different aspects of your dream state
throughout the day, usually the best
chance of recalling your dreams is when
you first awaken. And as you begin to
recall one of your dreams, relax and try to
remember how you *felt* during the dream
sequence, for recalling your *emotions*
will give you even more important
information than recalling the
details of your dream.

You must give
significant attention to
any subject for it to become
powerful enough to manifest in your
experience, and quite a bit of attention
must also be given to a subject before
it will begin to show up in your dream
state. For that reason, your more meaning-
ful dreams are always accompanied by
strong emotion; the emotion may feel
good or bad—but it will always be
strong enough so that you will
recognize the feeling.

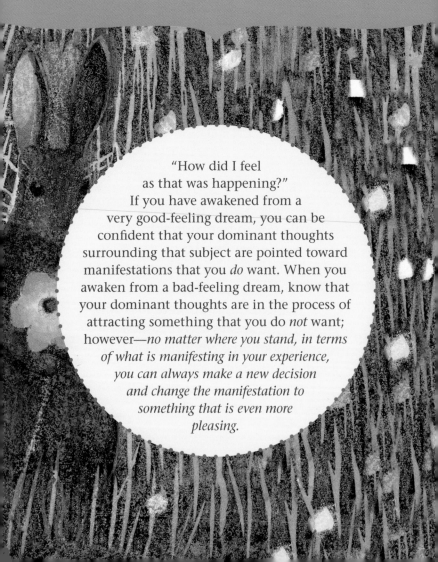

268

"How did I feel
as that was happening?"
If you have awakened from a
very good-feeling dream, you can be
confident that your dominant thoughts
surrounding that subject are pointed toward
manifestations that you *do* want. When you
awaken from a bad-feeling dream, know that
your dominant thoughts are in the process of
attracting something that you do *not* want;
however—*no matter where you stand, in terms
of what is manifesting in your experience,
you can always make a new decision
and change the manifestation to
something that is even more
pleasing.*

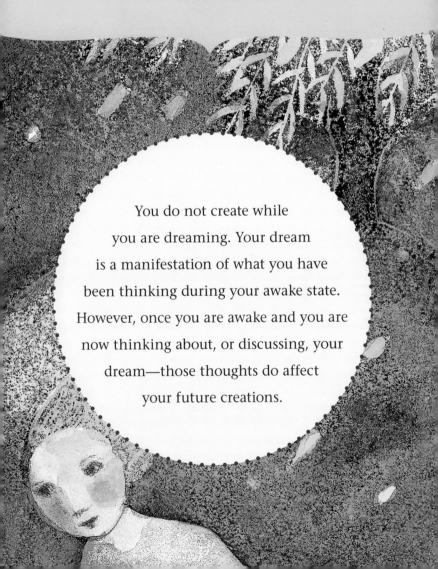

You do not create while
you are dreaming. Your dream
is a manifestation of what you have
been thinking during your awake state.
However, once you are awake and you are
now thinking about, or discussing, your
dream—those thoughts do affect
your future creations.

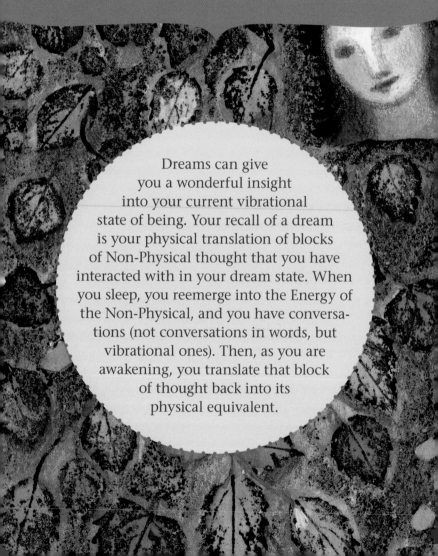

Dreams can give
you a wonderful insight
into your current vibrational
state of being. Your recall of a dream
is your physical translation of blocks
of Non-Physical thought that you have
interacted with in your dream state. When
you sleep, you reemerge into the Energy of
the Non-Physical, and you have conversations (not conversations in words, but
vibrational ones). Then, as you are
awakening, you translate that block
of thought back into its
physical equivalent.

Sometimes when you have
wanted something for a long while
but you do not see any way for it to
really happen, you will experience a
dream where it *does* happen. And then, in
the pleasant recollection of the dream,
you soften your vibration of
resistance—and then your
desire can be fulfilled.

Your dreams are
manifestations of your
vibrational point of attraction,
so you can evaluate your dreams to
determine what you are really doing
with your vibration. Your dreams are,
sort of, a sneak preview of the essence of
that which is to come—so if you evaluate
the content of your dream, you can often
determine what your point of attraction
is—and then if you do not wish to
live out the dream you have been
dreaming, you can do something about changing it.

273

As a result of
the influence surrounding
you, you may be flowing Energy
toward financial disaster, or toward a
body that will not function well. As such,
your *Inner Being,* which is aware of what you
are projecting into your future, may offer you
a dream showing you where you are going.
And so, you awaken and you think, *Ah, I don't
want that!* And then you say, *What is it I do
want? And why do I want it?* And then you
start flowing your Energy productively
toward what you do want, and
thereby changing your future
experience.

To begin the process of the *Book of Positive Aspects:* Purchase a notebook that feels good when you hold it in your hands. Because of the action that will be involved in this process, not only is an improved degree of focus certain, but with the focus will come an increase in both your clarity and in your feeling of being alive. Now, on the cover of your note-book write: *My Book of Positive Aspects.*

At the top of
the first page of your
Positive Aspects notebook, write
the name, or a brief description, of
someone or something that you always
feel good about. It could be the name of
your lovable cat, your best friend, or the
person you are in love with. It could be the
name of your favorite city or restaurant.
And as you focus upon the name or title
that you have written, ask yourself
these questions: *What do I like
about you? Why do I love you so
much? What are your
positive aspects?*

Gently and easily, begin writing down the thoughts that come to you in response to your *Positive Aspects* Questions. Do not try to force these ideas, but let them flow easily through you onto your paper. Write as long as the good-feeling thoughts flow, and then read what you have written, enjoying your own words. Now, turn to the next page and write another name or title of someone or something that you feel good about, and then repeat the process until about 20 minutes have passed.

The more *positive aspects* you search for, the more you are going to find; and the more *positive aspects* you find, the more you will search for more. In the *Book of Positive Aspects Process,* you will activate within yourself a high vibration of Well-Being (which matches who-you-really-are). And you will feel wonderful. And even better, this vibration will become so practiced that it will become your dominant vibration—and all aspects of your experience will now begin to reflect this higher vibration.

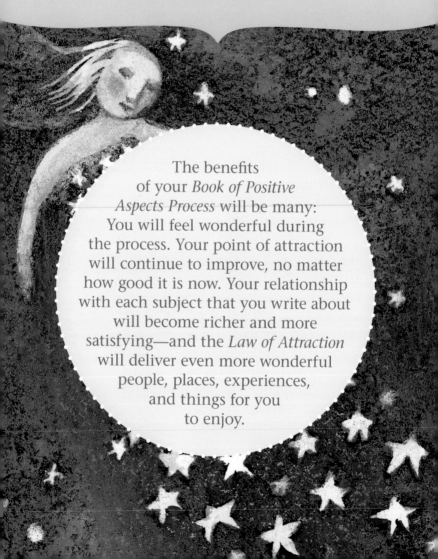

The benefits of your *Book of Positive Aspects Process* will be many: You will feel wonderful during the process. Your point of attraction will continue to improve, no matter how good it is now. Your relationship with each subject that you write about will become richer and more satisfying—and the *Law of Attraction* will deliver even more wonderful people, places, experiences, and things for you to enjoy.

If, when you
focus upon what you
want, you would feel good; and
if, when you feel good, you would
be in the positive mode of attraction,
then would not your most important
work be to look for the positive aspects
of all things, to look for the parts
of all things that are uplifting to
you—and to get your attention
off of any potholes in
the streets?

We want to encour-
age you to give more of your
attention to what makes you feel
good—not something so radical that
you must control every thought—*just
make a decision that you will look for what
you want to see.* It is not a difficult decision to make, but it can make a big
difference in what you bring
into your experience.

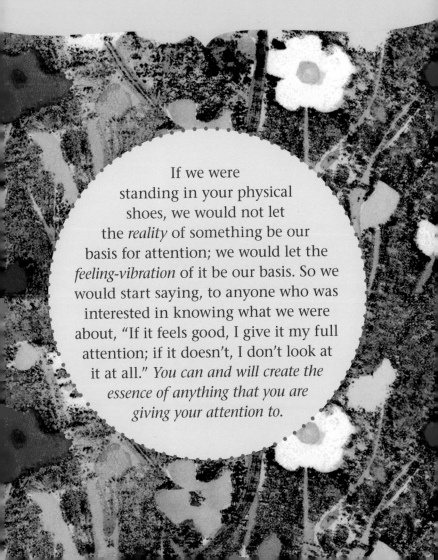

If we were
standing in your physical
shoes, we would not let
the *reality* of something be our
basis for attention; we would let the
feeling-vibration of it be our basis. So we
would start saying, to anyone who was
interested in knowing what we were
about, "If it feels good, I give it my full
attention; if it doesn't, I don't look at
it at all." *You can and will create the
essence of anything that you are
giving your attention to.*

You can look
at this in two different
ways: *If I do such and such, these
good things will happen*, or *If I don't
do such and such, these bad things will
happen*. The first *inspires* you to action
from a positive place. The second *moti-
vates* you to action from a negative place.
Your *Book of Positive Aspects* will put
you more and more in the position of
attracting—by virtue of your
inspired positive feeling—
whatever you desire.

This is how the *Scripting Process* works: Pretend that you are a writer and that whatever you write will be performed exactly as you write it. Your only job is to describe, in detail, everything, exactly as you want it to be.

The *Scripting Process* will help you be more specific about your desires, and, with that greater clarity about exactly what you *do* desire, you will feel the power of this specific focus. The longer you concentrate on a subject, and the more detail you give to it, the faster the Energy moves. And, with practice, you can actually *feel* the momentum of your desire; you can *feel* the Universal Forces converging. Often, you will be able to know when you are on the brink of a breakthrough or a manifestation just by virtue of the way you feel.

285

You are the
vibrational writer of the
script of your life—and everyone else in the Universe is playing
the part that you have assigned to
them. You can literally script any life
that you desire, and the Universe will
deliver to you the essence of the people,
places, and events just as you decide
them to be. For you are the creator
of your own experience—you
have only to decide it and
allow it to be.

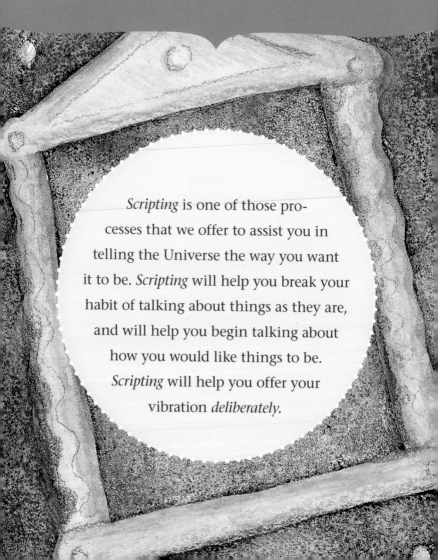

Scripting is one of those processes that we offer to assist you in telling the Universe the way you want it to be. *Scripting* will help you break your habit of talking about things as they are, and will help you begin talking about how you would like things to be. *Scripting* will help you offer your vibration *deliberately*.

If you regurgitate your script
often enough, you begin to accept
it as reality; and when you are accept-
ing it in the way you accept reality, the
Universe believes it and responds
in the same way.

In the moment
that you say "I prefer"
or "I like" or "I appreciate" or
"I want," the heavens part for you,
and the Non-Physical Energies, in that
instant, begin orchestrating the manifestation of your desire. In that instant! Faster
than you can speak it, the Energy begins to
flow, and circumstances and events (in an
orchestration that we cannot begin to
describe) begin to fall into place in order
to give you exactly what you want—
and if it were not for your resistance, things would happen
really fast.

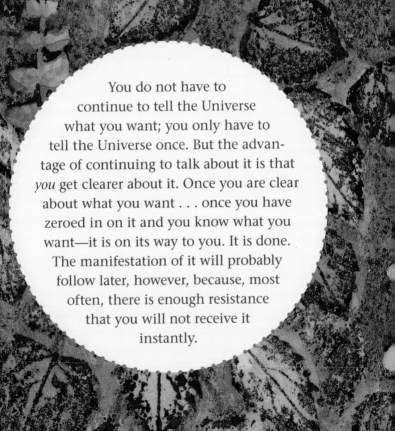

You do not have to
continue to tell the Universe
what you want; you only have to
tell the Universe once. But the advantage of continuing to talk about it is that
you get clearer about it. Once you are clear
about what you want . . . once you have
zeroed in on it and you know what you
want—it is on its way to you. It is done.
The manifestation of it will probably
follow later, however, because, most
often, there is enough resistance
that you will not receive it
instantly.

If you are experi-
encing a physical condition
that has your attention, you are,
through your attention to your current
condition, projecting it on into your future
experience. But, by focusing on a *different*
future experience, you are now activating
that *different* experience; and as you
project that changed experience into
your future, you leave your current experience behind.

You are
actually prepaving your
future experiences constantly
without even knowing you are doing
so. You are continually projecting your
expectations into your future experiences, and so a process of *Segment Intending* will help you to *consciously* consider
what you are projecting—and it will
help to give you control of your
future Segments.

You enter a new
Segment anytime your
intentions change: If you are
washing dishes and the telephone
rings, you enter a new Segment. When
you get into your vehicle, you enter a new
Segment. When another person walks into
the room, you enter a new Segment. If you will
take the time to get your thought of expectation started even before you are inside your
new Segment, you will be able to set the
tone of the Segment more specifically
than if you walk into the Segment
and begin to observe it as
it already is.

For some, you
may find it more efficient
and effective to carry a small notebook and physically stop and identify
the Segment while you write a list of your
intentions in your notebook—for as you are
writing, you will find yourself at your strongest point of clarity and at your strongest
point of focus—and so, in the beginning
of your deliberate *Segment Intending,*
you may find a notebook a very
great and valuable asset.

If you want many
things all at the same time,
it adds confusion. But when you
only focus upon the specifics of what
you want in any particular moment, you
bring to your creation clarity and power—
and therefore, speed. And that is the point of
Segment Intending: to stop, as you are entering
a new Segment, and to identify what it is you
most want so that you may give your attention to (and therefore draw power unto)
that. *Segment Intending* will put you in the
position of being a deliberate, magnetic
attractor, or creator, in each of
your Segments throughout
your day.

We encourage an application of the *Segment Intending Process* when you are already feeling good. If you are feeling bad, in this moment, do something else in order to improve your current mood and point of attraction. And then, once you are feeling better, you could return to this powerful *Segment Intending Process*.

The value of the
Segment Intending Process is
to encourage you to pause many
times during the day to say, "This
is what I want from this period of my
life experience. I want it and I expect
it." And as you set forth those powerful words, you become what we call
a *Selective Sifter*—you attract into
your experience what
you want.

As you are *Segment Intending* throughout a day, you will feel the power and the momentum of your intentions building; you will find yourself feeling gloriously invincible; you will feel as if there is nothing that you cannot be, do, or have as you are seeing yourself again and again in creative control of your own life experience.

When
you say, "I want
this thing to happen that
hasn't happened yet," you are
not only activating the vibration of
your desire, but you are also activating
a vibration of the absence of your
desire—so nothing changes for you.
And often, even when you do not speak
the second part of the sentence, and you
say only, "I want this to happen," there
is an unspoken vibration within you
that continues to hold you in a
state of not allowing
your desire.

When you say,
"Wouldn't it be nice if this
desire would come to me?" you
achieve an expectation that is much
less resistant in nature. Your question to
yourself naturally elicits from you a more
positive, expectant response. And so, this
simple but powerful game will cause a raising
of your vibration and an improvement in your
point of attraction because it naturally orients
you toward the things that you want. The
Wouldn't It Be Nice If . . . ? Process will
help you let in the things that you
have been asking for, on
all subjects.

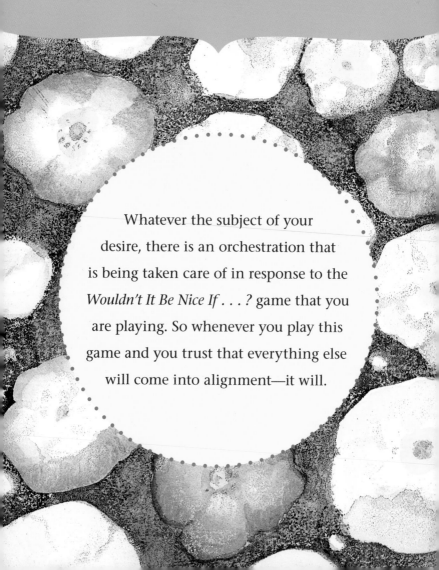

Whatever the subject of your desire, there is an orchestration that is being taken care of in response to the *Wouldn't It Be Nice If . . . ?* game that you are playing. So whenever you play this game and you trust that everything else will come into alignment—it will.

Every subject is
really two subjects: something that you desire, and the
absence of something that you desire.
If you do not understand that these are
very different vibrational frequencies, then
you may believe that you are focused on
something that you desire, when you
may, in fact, be focused in the
opposite direction.

302

Often, when you are interacting with others, you may be confused about whether the thought actually feels better to *you*, or whether you are offering it because you think it is the choice someone else would want you to make. *It is important to leave everyone else's ideas, desires, opinions, and beliefs aside while you identify, for yourself, how you feel.*

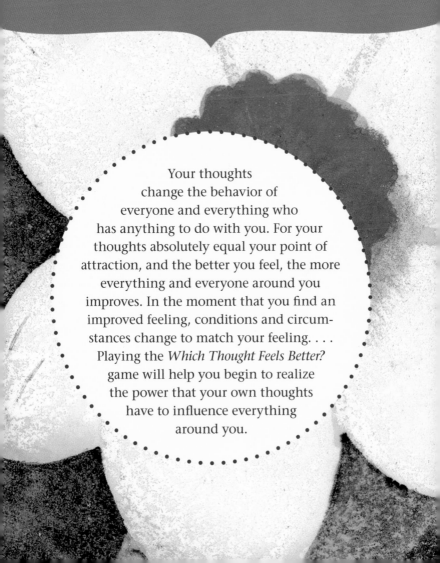

Your thoughts
change the behavior of
everyone and everything who
has anything to do with you. For your
thoughts absolutely equal your point of
attraction, and the better you feel, the more
everything and everyone around you
improves. In the moment that you find an
improved feeling, conditions and circumstances change to match your feeling. . . .
Playing the *Which Thought Feels Better?*
game will help you begin to realize
the power that your own thoughts
have to influence everything
around you.

304

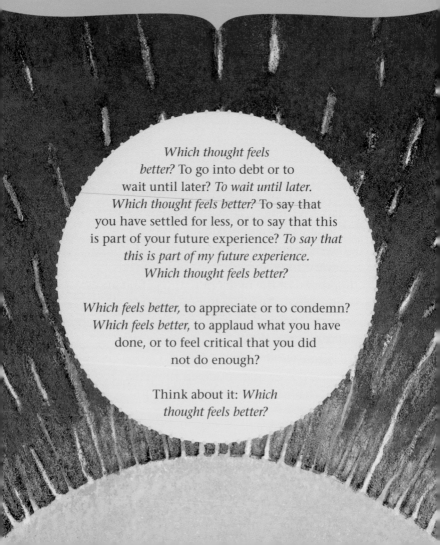

Which thought feels better? To go into debt or to wait until later? *To wait until later. Which thought feels better?* To say that you have settled for less, or to say that this is part of your future experience? *To say that this is part of my future experience. Which thought feels better?*

Which feels better, to appreciate or to condemn? *Which feels better,* to applaud what you have done, or to feel critical that you did not do enough?

Think about it: *Which thought feels better?*

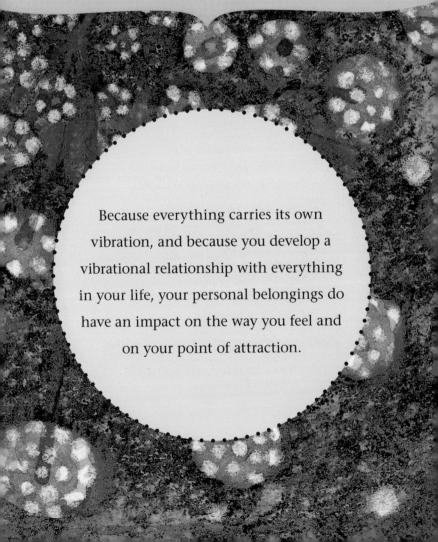

Because everything carries its own vibration, and because you develop a vibrational relationship with everything in your life, your personal belongings do have an impact on the way you feel and on your point of attraction.

Sometimes people will tell us that they are not bothered by clutter, so we tell them that the *Clearing Clutter Process* is, then, unnecessary for them. However, since every piece of everything does carry a vibration, almost everyone really does feel better in an uncluttered environment.

*Discard everything
from your experience that
is not essential to your <u>now.</u>* If you
could release those things you are not
wearing, release those things you are not
using—release them and leave your experience in a clearer place—then the things that
are more in harmony with who you are *now*
will more easily flow into your experience. *You
all have a capacity for attraction, and when your
process is clogged with stuff that you no longer
want, the new attraction is slower—and
then you end up with a feeling of
frustration or overwhelment.*

308

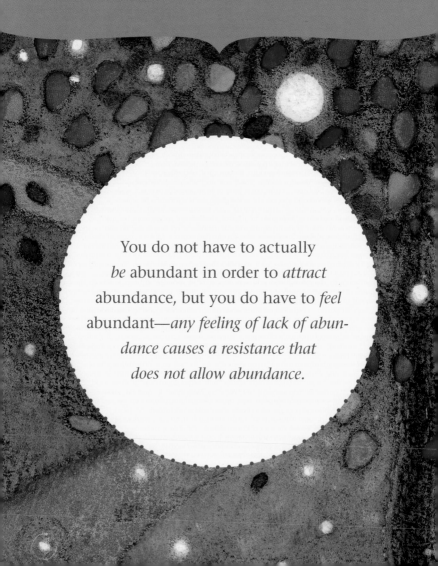

You do not have to actually *be* abundant in order to *attract* abundance, but you do have to *feel* abundant—*any feeling of lack of abundance causes a resistance that does not allow abundance.*

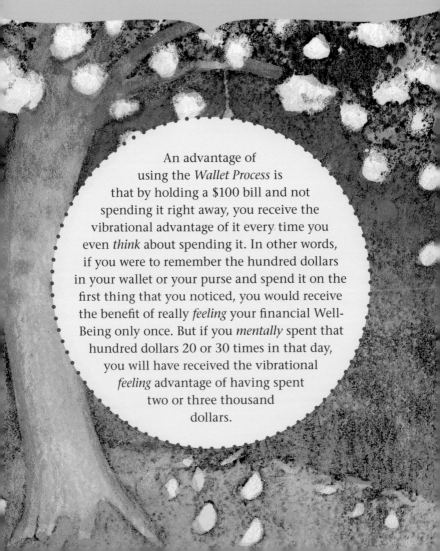

An advantage of
using the *Wallet Process* is
that by holding a $100 bill and not
spending it right away, you receive the
vibrational advantage of it every time you
even *think* about spending it. In other words,
if you were to remember the hundred dollars
in your wallet or your purse and spend it on the
first thing that you noticed, you would receive
the benefit of really *feeling* your financial Well-
Being only once. But if you *mentally* spent that
hundred dollars 20 or 30 times in that day,
you will have received the vibrational
feeling advantage of having spent
two or three thousand
dollars.

Seemingly magical things
will begin to occur as soon as you
achieve that wonderful feeling of
financial abundance: The money you are
currently earning will seem to go further.
Unexpected amounts of money in
various increments will begin to
show up in your experience.

311

You have to feel good about great
abundance before you will allow the
pleasure of great abundance to flow
into your experience.

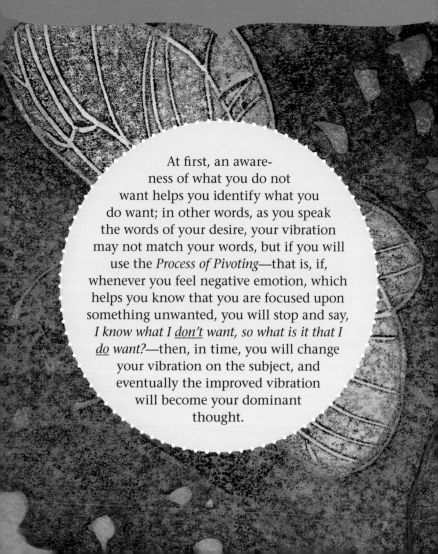

312

At first, an aware-
ness of what you do not
want helps you identify what you
do want; in other words, as you speak
the words of your desire, your vibration
may not match your words, but if you will
use the *Process of Pivoting*—that is, if,
whenever you feel negative emotion, which
helps you know that you are focused upon
something unwanted, you will stop and say,
*I know what I <u>don't</u> want, so what is it that I
<u>do</u> want?*—then, in time, you will change
your vibration on the subject, and
eventually the improved vibration
will become your dominant
thought.

It is possible to
be focused in vibrational
opposition to what you really
desire without knowing you are. It is
like the opposite ends of a stick. When
you pick up a stick, you pick up both ends.
The *Pivoting Process* will help you be more
aware of which end of your stick you are
currently activating: the end that is
about what you want, or the end
that is about the *absence* of
what you want.

See the *Process of
Pivoting* as a gradual shifting of your point of attraction, and
enjoy the positive results that must
follow. It is not possible for you to consistently give your attention to what you *do*
want and not receive it—for the *Law of
Attraction* guarantees that whatever you
are predominantly focused upon
will flow into your
experience.

The most important thing to remember is that you are the attractor of your experience, and that you are attracting it by virtue of the thoughts that you are offering. Thoughts are magnetic, and as you think a thought, it will attract another and another and another, until eventually you will have a physical manifestation of the vibrational essence of whatever has been the subject of your thoughts.

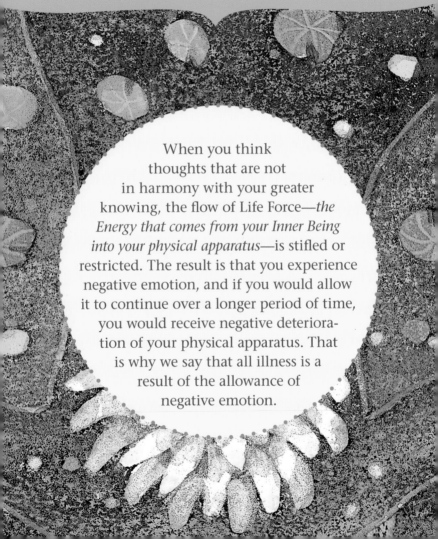

When you think
thoughts that are not
in harmony with your greater
knowing, the flow of Life Force—*the
Energy that comes from your Inner Being
into your physical apparatus*—is stifled or
restricted. The result is that you experience
negative emotion, and if you would allow
it to continue over a longer period of time,
you would receive negative deteriora-
tion of your physical apparatus. That
is why we say that all illness is a
result of the allowance of
negative emotion.

As you are
understanding that a
feeling of negative energy is an
indicator that you are not in harmony
with your greater knowing, many of you
have reached the point of saying, "I want to
feel good more of the time." And we say that
is a magnificent acknowledgment, because
when you are saying, "I want to feel good,"
what you are really saying is: "I want to be in
the place of positive attraction," or "I want
to be in a place where the thoughts that
I'm thinking as I'm feeling good are
in harmony with my greater
awareness."

Never are you
more clear about what you
do want than when experiencing
what you do not want. And so, if you
will stop and say, "Something is important
here, otherwise I would not be feeling this
negative emotion; I need to focus on what I
want," and then turn your attention to what
you *do* want . . . in that moment of turning
your attention, the negative emotion and
the negative attraction will stop—and the
positive attraction will begin—and your
feelings will change from not feeling
good to feeling good. *That is
the <u>Process of Pivoting.</u>*

When you feel
bad, you are in the process
of attracting something that
will not please you, and it is always
because you are focused upon the lack
of something you want. The *Process of
Pivoting* is the conscious decision to identify
what you *do* want. We do not want to imply
that the feeling of negative emotion is a bad
thing, because, very often, in the feeling of
negative emotion, you are alerted to the
fact that you are in the process of negatively attracting. And so, it is like a
"warning bell." It is part of your
*Emotional Guidance
System.*

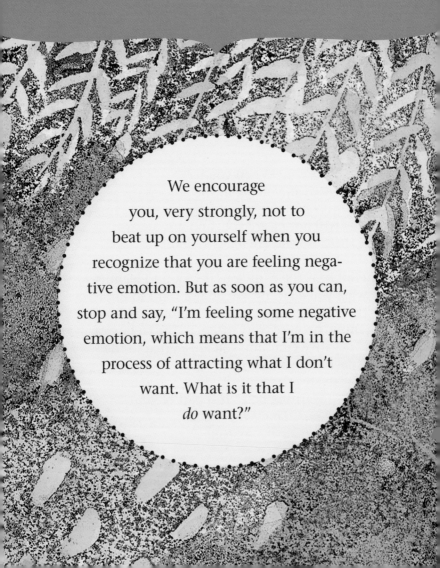

We encourage
you, very strongly, not to
beat up on yourself when you
recognize that you are feeling negative emotion. But as soon as you can,
stop and say, "I'm feeling some negative
emotion, which means that I'm in the
process of attracting what I don't
want. What is it that I
do want?"

321

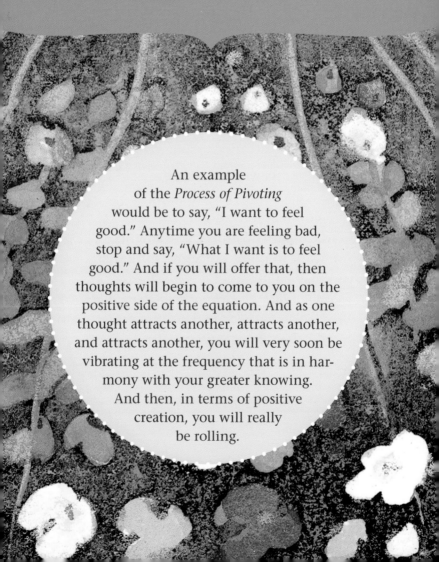

An example
of the *Process of Pivoting*
would be to say, "I want to feel
good." Anytime you are feeling bad,
stop and say, "What I want is to feel
good." And if you will offer that, then
thoughts will begin to come to you on the
positive side of the equation. And as one
thought attracts another, attracts another,
and attracts another, you will very soon be
vibrating at the frequency that is in harmony with your greater knowing.
And then, in terms of positive
creation, you will really
be rolling.

322

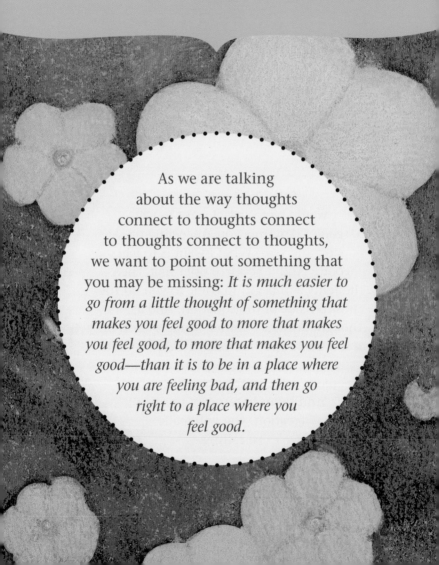

As we are talking
about the way thoughts
connect to thoughts connect
to thoughts connect to thoughts,
we want to point out something that
you may be missing: *It is much easier to
go from a little thought of something that
makes you feel good to more that makes
you feel good, to more that makes you feel
good—than it is to be in a place where
you are feeling bad, and then go
right to a place where you
feel good.*

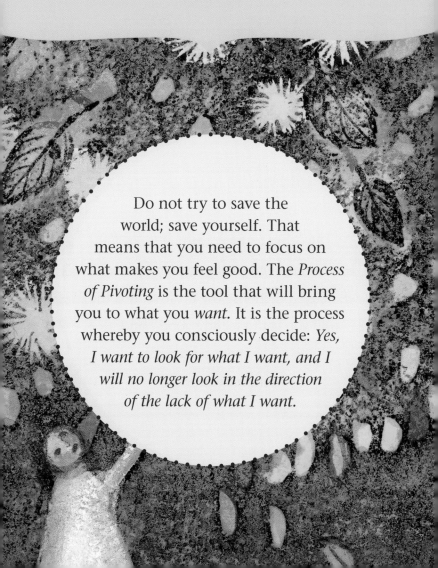

Do not try to save the world; save yourself. That means that you need to focus on what makes you feel good. The *Process of Pivoting* is the tool that will bring you to what you *want*. It is the process whereby you consciously decide: *Yes, I want to look for what I want, and I will no longer look in the direction of the lack of what I want.*

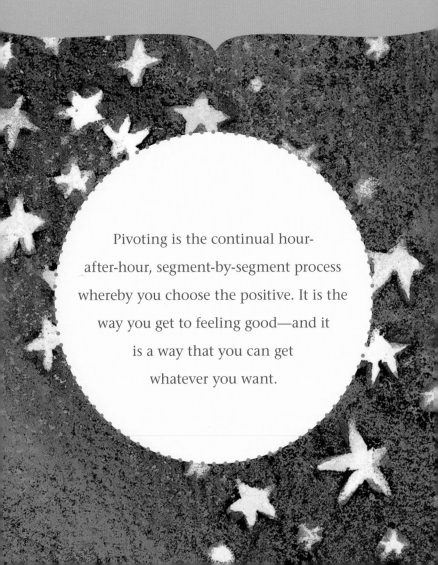

Pivoting is the continual hour-
after-hour, segment-by-segment process
whereby you choose the positive. It is the
way you get to feeling good—and it
is a way that you can get
whatever you want.

Sometimes some-
one will say to us, "But
Abraham, I cannot ignore this,
for it's true!" And we say, *It is only true
because someone has made it true by giving
their attention to it.* You see, what you are
actually saying here is, "Because someone
else has given attention to this and, therefore, by the *Law of Attraction,* invited it into
their own experience, I think I'll do the
same. In other words, even though I
don't want it, I'm obliged to create
it in my own reality because
someone else did."

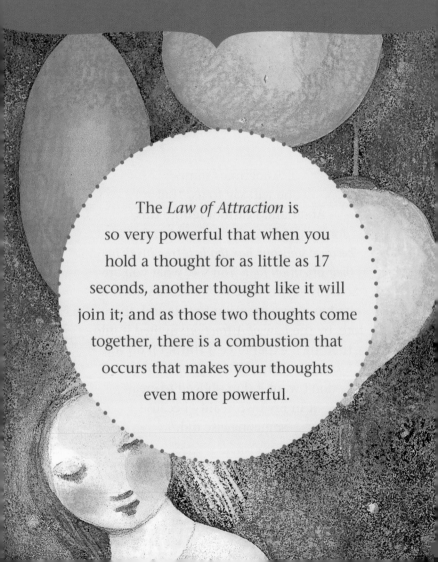

The *Law of Attraction* is
so very powerful that when you
hold a thought for as little as 17
seconds, another thought like it will
join it; and as those two thoughts come
together, there is a combustion that
occurs that makes your thoughts
even more powerful.

Your point of power is in the present because even though you may be thinking about the *past,* or you may be thinking about the *now,* or you may be thinking about the *future, you are doing it all right now.* You are vibrating *now.* The pulse is *now.* The vibrational offering is *now.* Any creative tension between the summoning of the Life Force and allowing it to flow through (the summoning and the allowing)—is all happening right here in the *now.*

Whether it is a castle or a button, if you are using it as your object of attention, it is summoning the Life Force—and it is the feel of the Life Force that life is about; the reason that you are summoning it is inconsequential. In other words, it is every bit as possible to feel as much joy in the preparation of your taxes as in the planning of an ocean cruise.

There is no value
in using happy-sounding
words if you do not *feel* happy.
The *Law of Attraction* is not responding to your words, but instead,
is responding to the vibrations that are
radiating from you. It is quite possible for
you to use all the right-sounding words at
the same time that you are in a state of
powerful resistance to your own Well-
Being, for the words you use are
not important—how you *feel*
is what matters.

As you focus upon what it *feels* like to be living your desire, you cannot, at the same time, be *feeling the absence* of your desire, so with practice, you can tip the scale, so to speak, so that even though your desire has not yet actually manifested, you are offering a vibration as if it has—and then it *must*.

The Universe does not know
if you are offering your vibration
because you are *living* what you are living, or because you are *imagining* that you
are living it. In either case, it answers
the vibration—and the manifestation
must follow.

Your intent, in the *Finding the Feeling-Place Process,* is to conjure images that cause you to offer a vibration that *allows* money. Your goal is to create images that *feel* good to you. Your goal is to find the *feeling-place* of what it would be like to have enough money rather than finding the *feeling-place* of what it is like to *not* have enough money.

The more often
you play the *Finding the
Feeling-Place Process,* the better
you will be at playing it, and the
more fun it will become. When you
pretend, or selectively remember, you
activate new vibrations—and your point
of attraction shifts. And when your
point of attraction shifts, your life will
improve regarding every subject
for which you have found a
new *feeling-place.*

334

There is nothing wrong
with debt, but if your debt feels
like a heavy burden, then your vibration around money is one of resistance.
When the burden has lifted, when you feel
lighter and freer, your resistance has lifted,
and you are now in the position to
allow the Well-Being to flow abun-
dantly into your experience.

It is as easy to
create a castle as a button.
It is just a matter of whether you
are focused on a castle or a button,
but it can also be as satisfying to create
a button as a castle. And whether it is a
castle or a button, if you are using it as your
object of attention, it is summoning the
Life Force, and the *feeling* of the Life
Force is what life is about; the reason
why you are summoning it is
inconsequential.

So, what about creating a very positive current of financial abundance? What about getting so good at visualizing that the money flows through you easily? What about spending money, and giving more people opportunity? What better way could anyone spend money than by putting it back into the economy that gives more people work? The more money you spend, the more people benefit, and the more people get in on the game and dovetail with you.

337

Your role is
to utilize Energy. That
is why you exist. You are an
Energy-flowing Being—a focuser, a
perceiver. You are a creator, and there
is nothing worse in all of the Universe
than to come forth into the environment of great contrast, where desire is
easily born, and not allow Energy
to flow to your desire—that is a
true squandering of life.

There is no "high work" or "low work." There are just opportunities to focus. You can feel as fulfilled and satisfied in any one task as in any other, for you are on the Leading Edge of thought, and Source is flowing through you no matter what your endeavor is. You can be joyful in any endeavor where you decide to allow the Energy to flow.

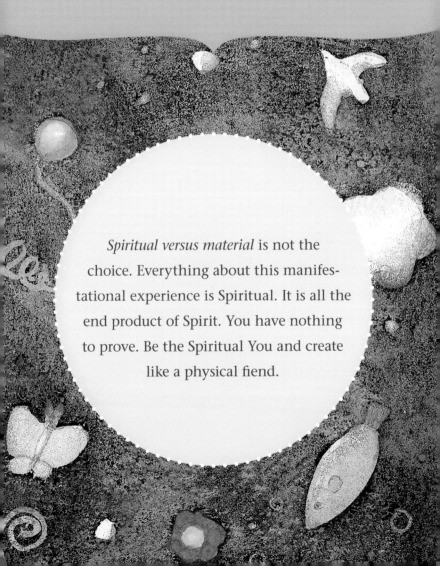

Spiritual versus material is not the choice. Everything about this manifestational experience is Spiritual. It is all the end product of Spirit. You have nothing to prove. Be the Spiritual You and create like a physical fiend.

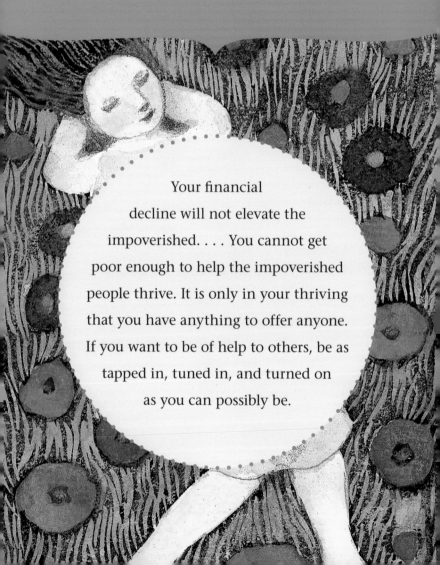

340

Your financial decline will not elevate the impoverished. . . . You cannot get poor enough to help the impoverished people thrive. It is only in your thriving that you have anything to offer anyone. If you want to be of help to others, be as tapped in, tuned in, and turned on as you can possibly be.

341

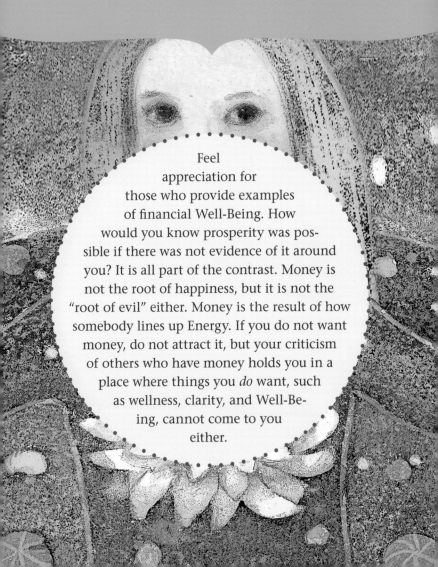

Feel appreciation for those who provide examples of financial Well-Being. How would you know prosperity was possible if there was not evidence of it around you? It is all part of the contrast. Money is not the root of happiness, but it is not the "root of evil" either. Money is the result of how somebody lines up Energy. If you do not want money, do not attract it, but your criticism of others who have money holds you in a place where things you *do* want, such as wellness, clarity, and Well-Being, cannot come to you either.

We love seeing you applauding someone else's success, because when you are genuinely thrilled by another's success, that means you are right on the track of your own. Many think *success* means getting everything they want. And we say that is what *dead* is, and there is no such thing as that kind of dead. Success is not about getting it done. It is about still dreaming and feeling positive in the unfolding. The standard of success in life is not the money or the stuff—rather, *it is absolutely the amount of joy you feel.*

343

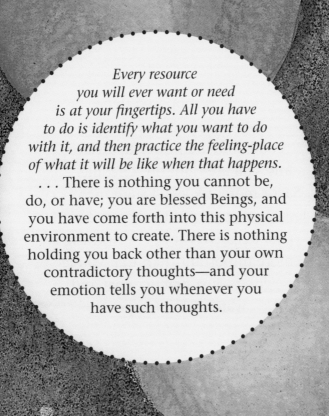

*Every resource
you will ever want or need
is at your fingertips. All you have
to do is identify what you want to do
with it, and then practice the feeling-place
of what it will be like when that happens.*
. . . There is nothing you cannot be,
do, or have; you are blessed Beings, and
you have come forth into this physical
environment to create. There is nothing
holding you back other than your own
contradictory thoughts—and your
emotion tells you whenever you
have such thoughts.

344

Life is supposed to be
fun—it is supposed to feel
good! You are powerful creators,
and you are right on schedule. . . .
Savor more; fix less. Laugh more; cry
less. Anticipate positively more; anticipate negatively less. . . . Nothing is
more important than that you feel
good—just practice that and
watch what happens.

You may be say-
ing to yourself, right now,
"I'd love to have a manager—
someone I can count on, someone
who would work on my behalf." And
we say to you, *You do have a manager
who is that and much more. You have a
"manager" who works continually on your
behalf called the* <u>Law of</u> <u>Attraction</u>—
*you have only to <u>ask</u> in order for your
Universal Manager to jump to
your request.*

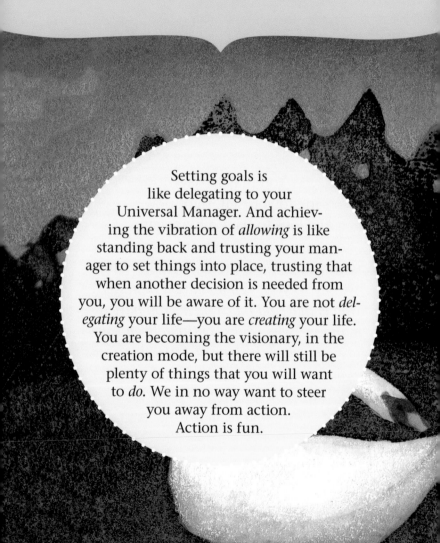

Setting goals is like delegating to your Universal Manager. And achieving the vibration of *allowing* is like standing back and trusting your manager to set things into place, trusting that when another decision is needed from you, you will be aware of it. You are not *delegating* your life—you are *creating* your life. You are becoming the visionary, in the creation mode, but there will still be plenty of things that you will want to *do*. We in no way want to steer you away from action. Action is fun.

There is not anything in all of the Universe more delicious than having a desire that you are a vibrational match to, and—in that alignment of your connection to Source Energy—being inspired to take an action. That is the furthest extension of the *Creation Process*—there is no action in all of the Universe more delicious than inspired action.

It is natural for your body to be well. And so, your goal is to be as comfortable as possible, and to breathe as deeply as you can while still remaining comfortable. There is nothing for you to do other than to relax and breathe. You will very likely begin to feel soft, gentle sensations in your body. Smile, and acknowledge that this is *Source Energy* specifically answering your cellular request. You are now *feeling* the healing process. Do nothing to try to help it or intensify it. Just relax and breathe—and allow it.

There is no
condition that you cannot
modify into something more,
any more than there is any paint-
ing that you cannot repaint. There are
many limiting thoughts in the human
environment that can make it seem that
these so-called incurable illnesses or
unchangeable conditions cannot be
changed—*but we say that they are
only "unchangeable" because
you believe they are.*

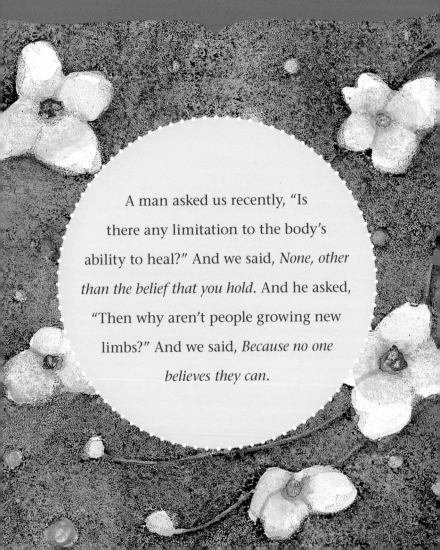

A man asked us recently, "Is there any limitation to the body's ability to heal?" And we said, *None, other than the belief that you hold.* And he asked, "Then why aren't people growing new limbs?" And we said, *Because no one believes they can.*

351

The question that
often arises is: "Well, what
about the little ones? What about
the unhealthy babies?" And we say
that they have been exposed to a vibration, even in the womb, which caused them
to disallow the Well-Being that would have
been there otherwise. But once they are born,
no matter what their disability, if they could
be encouraged to thoughts that would
allow the Well-Being, then even after
the body is fully formed, it could be
regenerated into something
that is well.

Do not let anyplace where
you are standing frighten you. All
it is, is a by-product of some Energy
alignment that only gives you stronger
clarity about what you want—and, most
important—greater sensitivity about
whether you are in a receiving mode
or locked off from it.

Wellness that is
being allowed, or wellness
that is being denied, is all about
the mind-set, the mood, the attitude,
or the practiced thoughts. There is not
one exception in any human or beast,
because you can patch them up again and
again—but they will just find another way
of reverting to the natural rhythm of
their mind. *Treating the body is really*
about treating the mind. It is all
psychosomatic—every bit of it.
No exceptions.

Any disease could be healed in a matter of days—yes, any disease—if distraction from it could occur and a different vibration dominate—and the healing time is about how much mix-up there is in all of that, for any malady in your physical body took a lot longer in coming than it takes to release it.

Do you have to think
specific positive thoughts about
your body in order for it to be the way
you want it to be? No. But you have to
not think the specific negative thoughts. If
you could never again think about your
body and, instead, just think pleasant
thoughts, your body would reclaim
its natural place of wellness.

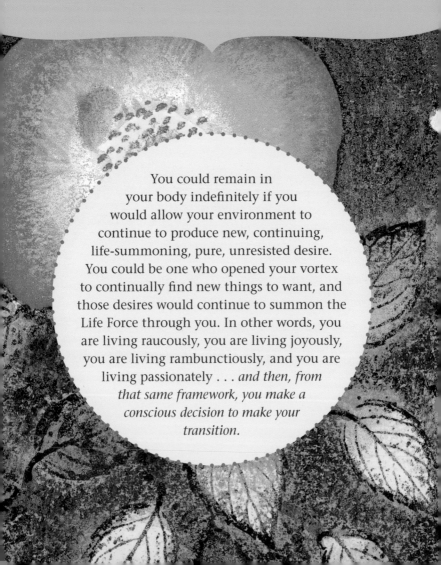

You could remain in
your body indefinitely if you
would allow your environment to
continue to produce new, continuing,
life-summoning, pure, unresisted desire.
You could be one who opened your vortex
to continually find new things to want, and
those desires would continue to summon the
Life Force through you. In other words, you
are living raucously, you are living joyously,
you are living rambunctiously, and you are
living passionately . . . *and then, from
that same framework, you make a
conscious decision to make your
transition.*

Every death is
brought about by the cul-
mination of the vibration of the
Being. There is not an exception to
that. No one, beast or human, makes
their transition into the Non-Physical
without it being the vibrational
consensus that is within them—
so every death is a suicide
because every death is
self-imposed.

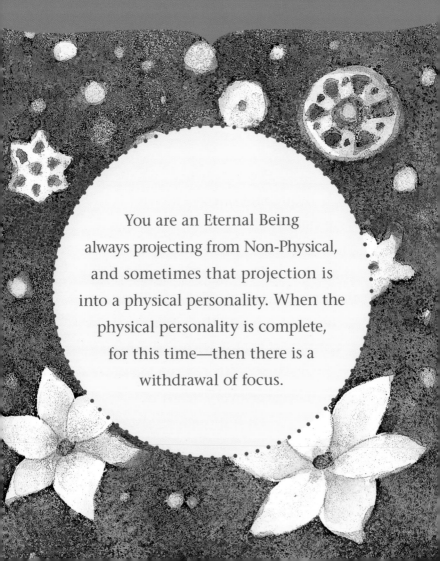

358

You are an Eternal Being
always projecting from Non-Physical,
and sometimes that projection is
into a physical personality. When the
physical personality is complete,
for this time—then there is a
withdrawal of focus.

359

If you believe
that something is good,
and you do it—it benefits you. If
you believe that something is bad,
and you do it—it is a very detrimental
experience. Get clear and happy about
whichever choice you make, because
it is your contradiction that causes
the majority of the contradiction in vibration.

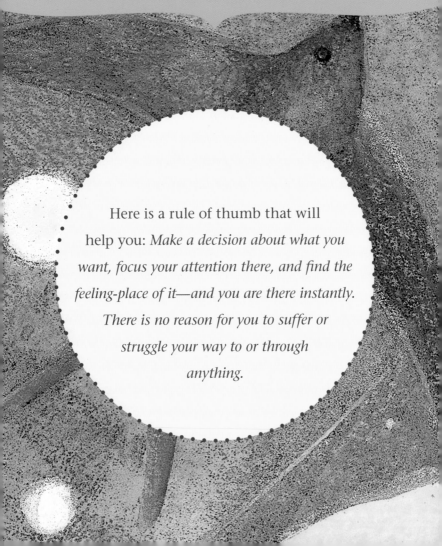

360

Here is a rule of thumb that will help you: *Make a decision about what you want, focus your attention there, and find the feeling-place of it—and you are there instantly. There is no reason for you to suffer or struggle your way to or through anything.*

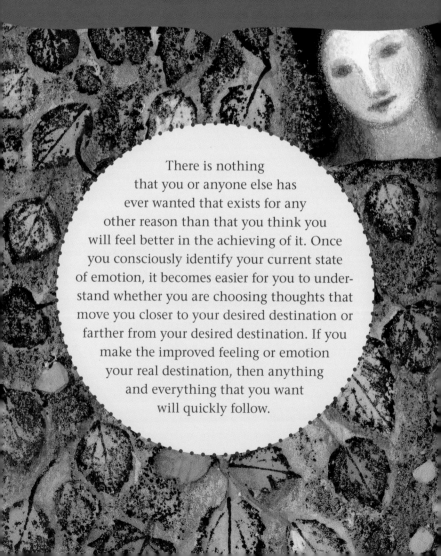

361

There is nothing
that you or anyone else has
ever wanted that exists for any
other reason than that you think you
will feel better in the achieving of it. Once
you consciously identify your current state
of emotion, it becomes easier for you to understand whether you are choosing thoughts that
move you closer to your desired destination or
farther from your desired destination. If you
make the improved feeling or emotion
your real destination, then anything
and everything that you want
will quickly follow.

Finding the
perfect word to describe the
way you feel is not essential to a
Moving-Up-the-Emotional-Scale Process,
but feeling the emotion is important—
and finding ways to improve the feeling
is even more important. In other words,
this game is strictly about discovering
thoughts that give you feelings
of relief.

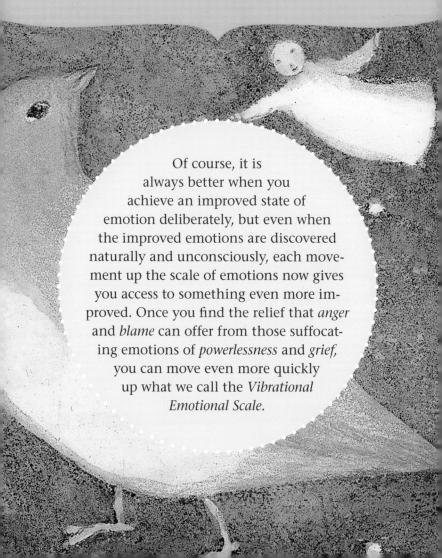

363

Of course, it is
always better when you
achieve an improved state of
emotion deliberately, but even when
the improved emotions are discovered
naturally and unconsciously, each move-
ment up the scale of emotions now gives
you access to something even more improved. Once you find the relief that *anger*
and *blame* can offer from those suffocat-
ing emotions of *powerlessness* and *grief,*
you can move even more quickly
up what we call the *Vibrational
Emotional Scale.*

Now that you
understand that your intent
is simply to reach a better-feeling
emotion, it is our expectation that the
Moving-Up-the-Emotional-Scale Process will
free you from troubling negative emotions that
you have been experiencing for years. And as
you gently and gradually release the resistance
you have unknowingly gathered, you will
begin to experience improvements in
your life experiences . . . in all
troubling areas of your life.

365

Be easy about all of this. Life
is supposed to be fun, you know. It
is our powerful desire that you return to
your state of self-appreciation. We want
you to feel love for your life, for the
people of your world, and, most of all,
for yourself.

ABOUT THE AUTHORS

Esther and Jerry Hicks, the *New York Times* best-selling authors of *Ask and It Is Given, The Amazing Power of Deliberate Intent, The Astonishing Power of Emotions,* and *The Law of Attraction*, produce the Leading Edge Abraham-Hicks teachings on the art of allowing our natural Well-Being to come forth. While presenting open workshops in up to 60 cities per year, the Hickses have now published more than 700 Abraham-Hicks books, CDs, and DVDs.

Their internationally acclaimed Website is: **www.abraham-hicks.com.**

HAY HOUSE TITLES
OF RELATED INTEREST

Healing Words from the Angels, by Doreen Virtue, Ph.D.

Never Mind Success . . . Go for Greatness! by Tavis Smiley

101 Ways to Jump-Start Your Intuition, by John Holland

The Present Moment, by Louise L. Hay

Vitamins for the Soul, by Sonia Choquette

Your Ultimate Calling, by Dr. Wayne W. Dyer

డ్రా

All of the above are available at your local
bookstore, or may be ordered by visiting:

Hay House USA: **www.hayhouse.com**®
Hay House Australia: **www.hayhouse.com.au**
Hay House UK: **www.hayhouse.co.uk**
Hay House South Africa: **www.hayhouse.co.za**
Hay House India: **www.hayhouse.co.in**

NOTES

NOTES

NOTES

NOTES

NOTES

We hope you enjoyed this Hay House Lifestyles book. If you'd like
to receive a free catalog featuring additional Hay House books and products,
or if you'd like information about the Hay Foundation, please contact:

Hay House, Inc.
P.O. Box 5100
Carlsbad, CA 92018-5100

(760) 431-7695 or **(800) 654-5126**
(760) 431-6948 (fax) or **(800) 650-5115 (fax)**
www.hayhouse.com® • **www.hayfoundation.org**

Published and distributed in Australia by:
Hay House Australia Pty. Ltd., 18/36 Ralph St., Alexandria NSW 2015
Phone: 612-9669-4299 • *Fax:* 612-9669-4144 • www.hayhouse.com.au

Published and distributed in the United Kingdom by:
Hay House UK, Ltd., 292B Kensal Rd., London W10 5BE
Phone: 44-20-8962-1230 • *Fax:* 44-20-8962-1239 • www.hayhouse.co.uk

Published and distributed in the Republic of South Africa by:
Hay House SA (Pty), Ltd., P.O. Box 990, Witkoppen 2068
Phone/Fax: 27-11-467-8904 • orders@psdprom.co.za • www.hayhouse.co.za

Published in India by: Hay House Publishers India,
Muskaan Complex, Plot No. 3, B-2, Vasant Kunj, New Delhi 110 070
Phone: 91-11-4176-1620 • *Fax:* 91-11-4176-1630 • www.hayhouse.co.in

Distributed in Canada by: Raincoast,
9050 Shaughnessy St., Vancouver, B.C. V6P 6E5
Phone: (604) 323-7100 • *Fax:* (604) 323-2600 • www.raincoast.com

Tune in to **HayHouseRadio.com®** for the best in inspirational talk radio
featuring top Hay House authors! And, sign up via the Hay House USA
Website to receive the Hay House online newsletter and stay informed
about what's going on with your favorite authors. You'll receive bimonthly
announcements about: Discounts and Offers, Special Events, Product
Highlights, Free Excerpts, Giveaways, and more!
www.hayhouse.com®